crochet chic

crochet chic

HAUTE CROCHET SCARVES, HATS & BAGS

FRANCINE TOUKOU

LARK BOOKS

A Division of Sterling Publishing Co., Inc.

New York / London

SENIOR EDITOR

VALERIE SHRADER

TECHNICAL EDITOR

K.J. HAY

ART DIRECTOR

STACEY BUDGE

COVER DESIGNER

CINDY LABREACHT

ASSISTANT EDITOR

NATHALIE MORNU

ASSOCIATE DESIGNER

TRAVIS MEDFORD

ART PRODUCTION ASSISTANT

JEFF HAMILTON

EDITORIAL ASSISTANCE

DAWN DILLINGHAM
CASSIE MOORE

ILLUSTRATOR

ORRIN LUNDGREN

PHOTOGRAPHER

STEWART O'SHIELDS

STYLIST

E. SCOTT THOMPSON

Library of Congress Cataloging-in-Publication Data

Toukou, Francine.
  Crochet chic : haute crochet scarves, hats & bags / Francine Toukou. --
1st ed.
    p. cm.
  Includes index.
  ISBN-13: 978-1-60059-078-8 (hc-plc with jacket : alk. paper)
  ISBN-10: 1-60059-078-0 (hc-plc with jacket : alk. paper)
  1. Crocheting--Patterns. 2. Clothing and dress. 3. Dress
accessories--Patterns. I. Title.
  TT825.T58 2007
  746.43'4041--dc22

                    2007016565

10 9 8 7 6 5 4 3 2 1

First Edition

Published by Lark Books, A Division of
Sterling Publishing Co., Inc.
387 Park Avenue South, New York, N.Y. 10016

Text © 2007, Francine Toukou
Photography © 2007, Lark Books unless otherwise specified
Illustrations © 2007, Lark Books unless otherwise specified

Distributed in Canada by Sterling Publishing,
c/o Canadian Manda Group, 165 Dufferin Street
Toronto, Ontario, Canada M6K 3H6

Distributed in the United Kingdom by GMC Distribution Services,
Castle Place, 166 High Street, Lewes, East Sussex, England BN7 1XU

Distributed in Australia by Capricorn Link (Australia) Pty Ltd.,
P.O. Box 704, Windsor, NSW 2756 Australia

If you have questions or comments about this book, please contact:
Lark Books
67 Broadway
Asheville, NC 28801
(828) 253-0467

Manufactured in China

ISBN 13: 978-1-60059-078-8
ISBN 10: 1-60059-078-0

For information about custom editions, special sales, premium and corporate purchases, please contact Sterling Special Sales Department at 800-805-5489 or specialsales@sterlingpub.com.

table of contents

introduction

A CROCHETED PIECE IS THE LOVELY MANIFESTATION of a thought, expressed through hand, heart, hook, and yarn. Crochet has always been a joyful and rewarding outlet for me. Most folks don't believe me when I tell them, but my mom will attest to the fact that she taught me how to crochet when I was three years old. I don't mention this tidbit of info in an attempt to boast. I simply offer it as proof that crochet is so easy and accessible even a three-year-old can do it! If you have never done it before, believe me when I say that you can learn.

I crocheted off and on throughout my childhood, but I really began to immerse myself in the craft when I was working as a hairstylist in the fashion and entertainment industry. I've owned hair salons for the past 15 years, and during that time I have worked as a stylist on the sets of many television programs, including *The View, Live with Regis & Kelly, The Rosie O'Donnell Show, The Cosby Show,* and *Late Show with David Letterman,* to name a few. I've also had the pleasure of working with fashion industry icons such as Catherine Malandrino, Annie Leibovitz, Peter Beard, and Naomi Campbell. Additionally, I've toured around the world with various recording artists. Oddly enough, although I've worked with this crowded cast of extroverted entertainers, I am one of the most introverted people I know. During down times on the set, while others shared tales of life in the fast lane, I had two options: I could sit around and twiddle my thumbs, or I could purpose all 10 of my digits in a twiddling of hook and yarn. Needless to say, I chose the latter option, and what happened was really surprising—I became the life of the party! As I crocheted, I began to work up lovely little ice-breaking conversation pieces, and almost everyone wanted in on the action.

Since that time, I literally have been unable to "unhook" myself (if you'll pardon the pun). From all those long hours on sets and in airports, I've compiled the 30 stylish yet easy projects in *Crochet Chic* in the hopes that you'll get hooked too. You'll see the influence of my background as a stylist in the unique color palette I'm fond of using, as well as the embellishments I add such as ruffles, crocheted flowers, and appliqués. Further, my designs offer a playful use of scale, with everything from short lacy scarves to the longest scarf you've ever seen, which I mischievously call *Get Lost.* I've also included a variety of yarns to suit every aesthetic and pocketbook, and you'll learn all about the basics of crochet. Remember—even a three-year-old can do it!

It is my belief that we all have the opportunity to experience the joy of creativity. Crochet is my artistic outlet. I hope you'll be inspired by these crocheted accessories and will enjoy making the projects as much as I enjoyed designing them.

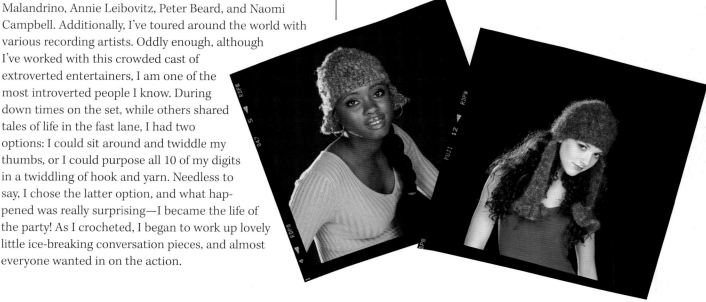

the art
of crochet

CROCHET IS AN ACCESSIBLE ART that comes with a license to be prolific. At the same time, however, you can create beautiful pieces using simple stitches and patterns. It need not be a complicated craft.

Crochet is very much about the finished product, but in many ways, it's also about the journey or act itself. When embarking on any journey, it is a good idea to do three things. First, be prepared; second, pack light; and third, enjoy the ride!

In an effort to be prepared and well tooled, it's very tempting to pick up one of everything you find at your local craft or yarn store. While almost all tools and notions are useful, all you really need to produce any of the pieces featured in this book are the following: the right hook, some luscious yarn, a yarn needle, a ruler or measuring tape, a small pair of scissors, a love of the art, and of course, the patterns featured in *Crochet Chic*.

GETTING HOOKED

There's an overwhelming array of crochet hooks available today and just as many arguments for which type of hook is best. "Green hookers" prefer bamboo because it is natural, but other hookers like it because it tends to hook smoothly. "Happy hookers" like colorful, clear plastic hooks thanks to the cheerful variety of hues you can buy them in. There are those who like vintage and those who like bone, wood, pewter, or aluminum. There is even a school of crocheters who insist on the good old-fashioned index finger. I like to call myself a "convenience hooker," which means I grab whatever type of hook is available and conveniently get on with the business of hooking.

Experiment with the many different types of hooks available, and decide which one works best for you.

GAUGE

While there is room for flexibility in choosing your favorite type of hook, there are greater constraints when deciding on the size of hook necessary for a particular project.

The patterns featured in this book offer a suggested hook size, but the actual size of hook that you will use, will be determined by your own individual tension, or how tightly you make your stitches. The range of hook sizes needed for the projects in this book are as follows:

SIZE 3 OR D, WHICH IS 3.25 MILLIMETERS

SIZE 7 OR G, WHICH IS 4.5 MILLIMETERS

SIZE 8 OR H, WHICH IS 5 MILLIMETERS

SIZE 9 OR I, WHICH IS 5.5 MILLIMETERS

SIZE 10 OR J, WHICH IS 6 MILLIMETERS

SIZE 10.5 OR K, WHICH IS 6.5 MILLIMETERS

SIZE 15 OR N, WHICH IS 10 MILLIMETERS

In order to determine which size hook you need for a particular project, you will need to accurately measure the gauge of your stitches. This is done by making a gauge swatch. A gauge swatch is generally a 4 x 4-inch (10 x 10cm) square that is composed horizontally by a number of stitches, and vertically by a number of rows.

Make a gauge swatch using a hook of the size listed in the project. If the number of stitches in your gauge swatch is greater than the number of stitches in the suggested gauge of the pattern, you need to use a larger hook. If the number of stitches in your gauge swatch is less than the number of stitches in the suggested gauge of the pattern, you need to use a smaller hook.

THE YARN STORY

The fiber used to make yarn ranges from traditional sheep's wool to luxurious cashmere, simple acrylic, and recycled soy. Each fiber has its own special qualities. Wool is warm, cashmere is soft, acrylic is inexpensive and almost indestructible, and soy silk has a lovely sheen and appeals to the environmentally conscious. One of the delights of crochet is trying different types of yarn and learning how to best use the qualities of each type.

When it comes to yarn, I am by no means a purist, nor am I a yarn snob. So much of the beauty of crochet lies in its accessibility. You don't have to spend a fortune to get started, although you're welcome to, if you so desire. One of the loveliest and most appreciated gifts I ever whipped up was a granny square tote that I made with a batch of closeout acrylic purchased from a discount store.

On the flip side, I also enjoy the occasional splurge on yummy yarn (I told you I wasn't a purist). When working a potential heirloom piece for a newborn or lovingly hooking a cozy scarf to warm and embrace the neck of a loved one, why not yum it up and milk the occasion for all it's worth! Take the whole day to visit a high-end yarn boutique or café and ride high on the joyful experience of fingering through bales of hand-spun mohair and baby-soft alpaca. Even better, when the shopping is done, and you're sitting in your favorite chair in the warm glowing light of a crackling fire (or while you're riding on a crowded subway, like I often do), you'll be able to relive the joy of that day as you work it into each stitch of your crocheted piece.

The pattern instructions indicate the weight of yarn to be used. The details of the specific yarns used in each project are also provided. You may choose to use the specific yarns listed, or you may choose to substitute different yarns.

Yarns can be grouped into six categories by weight: super fine, fine, light, medium, bulky, and super bulky. Unfortunately, there are many different names in use for each of these weight categories (e.g. medium weight is more commonly called worsted weight) and two different yarns in the same weight category

may not have exactly the same weight or thickness. So it is always smart to select a yarn that is in the suggested weight category for the project you wish to make, but please be aware that this doesn't guarantee that your finished project will be the same size or have the same drape as the same project made with a different yarn. Not all the news is bad, however. Using a different yarn results in a unique piece, and often I've found that I prefer the slightly different size or drape of my results!

To be sure that your selected yarn will yield the desired project size, make a gauge swatch using the suggested hook size and yarn weight for the project. If you need to adjust the hook size (see above), make another swatch. Then, if you like the look and drape, go for it! Remember that a slightly smaller or larger scarf or tote is not usually a problem and in fact may suit your personal taste.

THE REST OF THE STORY

To complete your tool kit for the projects, you will also need a yarn needle, a ruler or measuring tape, and a small pair of scissors. A yarn needle is a large-eyed needle of plastic or metal. Tapestry and darning needles can substitute for a yarn needle.

JUST IN CASE...

If you need to brush up on the basics of crochet (stitches, stitch patterns, and so on), see Let's Get Technical on page 105.

the projects

Release your inner fashionista with the chic accessories that follow. Buy some beautiful yarn and spend a few hours creating an elegant mohair scarf, a funky felted bag, or a cool flapper hat—whatever your heart desires. Indulge yourself!

chunky char-cowl

Bring out your secret diva with this glamorous cowl. The sturdy and striking ribbing effect results when two strands of yarn are held together and the stitches are worked in the back loops only.

FINISHED MEASUREMENTS
20" long x 20" circumference/
51cm x 51cm

YOU WILL NEED
250yd/229m of worsted weight yarn in dark gray (A)

250yd/229m of worsted weight yarn in light gray (B)

Hook: 6.5mm/K-10.5 or size needed to obtain gauge

Yarn needle

STITCHES USED
Chain (ch)

Half double crochet (hdc)

GAUGE
Take time to check your gauge.

11 hdc = 4"/10cm

6½ rows = 4"/10cm

PATTERN NOTES
To create the rib stitch effect, the cowl is worked using half double crochet stitches worked in the back loops only.

The cowl is worked holding 1 strand each of A and B together throughout.

COWL

Holding 1 strand each of A and B together, ch 56.

Row 1: Hdc in 3rd ch from hook and in each ch across (54 sts).

Row 2: Ch 2, turn, working in back loops only, hdc in each hdc across.

Repeat Row 2 until piece measures 20"/51cm. Fasten off, leaving a 45"/114cm end for seaming.

FINISHING

Fold the finished rectangle in half, bringing first row to meet last row. Use long end of yarn to whipstitch edges together. Fasten off and weave in all yarn ends.

THIS PROJECT WAS CREATED WITH

Coats & Clark's Red Heart Classic, 100% acrylic, 3.5oz/99g = 190yd/174m

(A) 2 balls, color nickel (#401)

Lion Brand's Wool-Ease Worsted Weight, 80% acrylic, 20% wool, 3oz/85g = 197yd/180m

(B) 2 balls, color oxford grey (#152)

garden lady

Let Mother Nature have a little attitude when you wear this garden-inspired scarf. Its warm brown hue is adorned with simple but colorful crochet flowers.

FINISHED MEASUREMENTS

7" wide x 34" long/18cm x 86cm

YOU WILL NEED

180yd/165m of bulky weight yarn in brown (A)

40yd/37m of worsted weight yarn in green (B)

40yd/37m of worsted weight yarn in pink (C)

40yd/37m of worsted weight yarn in orange (D)

40yd/37m of worsted weight yarn in yellow (E)

40yd/37m of worsted weight yarn in brown (F)

Hooks: 5.5mm/I-9 and 10mm/N-15 or size needed to obtain gauge

Yarn needle

STITCHES USED

Chain (ch)

Half double crochet (hdc)

Double crochet (dc)

Single crochet (sc)

Slip stitch (sl st)

GAUGE

Take time to check your gauge.

10 dc = 4"/10cm with larger hook

6 rows = 4"/10cm with larger hook

1 Flower = 3"/8cm diameter with smaller hook

PATTERN NOTES

Double crochet stitches are worked in the spaces between stitches, not in the tops of stitches. The last space is between the last stitch and the beginning chain of the previous row.

SCARF

With larger hook and A, ch 20.

Row 1: Hdc in 3rd ch from hook and in each ch across (18 hdc).

Row 2: Ch 3 (counts as first dc here and throughout), turn, dc in each space between sts across (18 dc).

Row 3: Ch 2, turn, hdc in each space between sts across.

Repeat Rows 2 and 3 until piece measures 34"/86cm. Fasten off.

FLOWER

(make 5, 1 each with B, C, D, E, and F)

With smaller hook, ch 3; join with sl st in first ch to form a ring.

Rnd 1: Ch 3 (counts as first dc here and throughout), work 7 more dc in ring; join with sl st in top of beginning ch-3 (8 dc).

Rnd 2: Ch 5 (counts as dc, ch 2), *dc in next dc, ch 2; repeat from * around; join with sl st in 3rd ch of beginning ch-5 (8 ch-2 spaces).

Rnd 3 (back petals): Sl st into first ch-2 space, (sc, hdc, 3 dc, hdc, sc) in each ch-2 space around (8 petals).

Rnd 4: Working in front of Rnd 3 petals, *sl st around post of next dc of Rnd 1, ch 2; repeat from * around; join with sl st in first sl st (8 ch-2 spaces).

Rnd 5 (middle petals): Repeat Rnd 3 (8 petals).

Rnd 6: Working in front of Rnd 5 petals, sl st into ring between next 2 sts of Rnd 1, ch 2, *skip next st of Rnd 1, sl st into ring between next 2 sts of Rnd 1, ch 2; repeat from * around; join with sl st in first sl st (4 ch-2 spaces).

Rnd 7 (front petals): Repeat Rnd 3 (4 petals). Fasten off, leaving a 12"/31cm end for sewing.

FINISHING

Using photograph as a guide, sew flowers to scarf. Weave in all yarn ends.

THIS PROJECT WAS CREATED WITH

Lion Brand's Wool-Ease Thick & Quick, 80% acrylic, 20% wool, 6oz/170g = 106yd/97m

(A) 2 balls, color wood (#404)

Karabella's Aurora 8, 100% extra fine merino, 1.75oz/50g = 98yd/90m

(B) 1 ball, color #24

(C) 1 ball, color #62

(D) 1 ball, color #704

(E) 1 ball, color #17

(F) 1 ball, color #36

calico scarf and flower pin

Soften your power suit with this charming accessory. You'll speed through this project holding two strands of yarn together and working pairs of double crochets in the spaces between stitches.

PATTERN NOTES
Scarf is worked holding 1 strand each of A and B together throughout.

Flower is worked using a single strand of yarn.

Double crochet stitches are worked in the spaces between stitches, not in the top of stitches. The last space is between the last stitch and the beginning chain of the previous row.

SCARF

Holding 1 strand each of A and B together, ch 11.

Row 1: Hdc in 3rd ch from hook and in each ch across (9 hdc).

Row 2: Ch 3 (counts as first dc here and throughout), turn, *skip next space between sts, 2 dc in next space between sts; repeat from * across to last space, skip last space, dc in top of beginning ch-2.

Row 3: Ch 3, turn, *skip next space between sts, 2 dc in next space between sts; repeat from * across to last space, skip last space, dc in top of beginning ch-3.

Repeat Row 3 until piece measures 34"/86cm. Fasten off.

FLOWER

With 1 strand of C, ch 3; join with sl st in first ch to form a ring.

Rnd 1: Ch 3 (counts as first dc here and throughout), work 8 more dc in ring; join with sl st in top of beginning ch-3 (9 dc).

Rnd 2: Ch 5 (counts as dc, ch 2), *dc in next dc, ch 2; repeat from * around; join with sl st in 3rd ch of beginning ch-5 (9 ch-2 spaces). Fasten off.

Rnd 3: Join 1 strand of D with sc in any ch-2 space, (hdc, 3 dc, hdc, sc) in same ch-2 space, (sc, hdc, 3 dc, hdc, sc) in each ch-2 space around (9 petals). Fasten off.

Rnd 4: Working in front of Rnd 3 petals, join 1 strand of C with sl st around the post of any dc of Rnd 2, ch 3, *sl st around post of next dc of Rnd 2, ch 3; repeat from * around; join with sl st in join (9 ch-3 spaces). Fasten off.

Rnd 5: Join 1 strand of D with sc in any ch-3 space, (hdc, 2 dc, hdc, sc) in same ch-3 space, (sc, hdc, 2 dc, hdc, sc) in each ch-3 space around (9 petals). Fasten off.

FINISHING

Weave in all yarn ends. With 1 strand of D, whipstitch flower to brooch pin. Use flower pin as closure for scarf.

THIS PROJECT WAS CREATED WITH

Lion Brand's Wool-Ease Worsted Weight, 80% acrylic, 20% wool, 3oz/85g = 197yd/180m.

(A) 1 ball, color cocoa (#129)

(B) 1 ball, color fisherman (#099)

Coats & Clark's Red Heart Classic, 100% acrylic, 3.5oz/99g = 190yd/174m.

(C) 1 ball, color coffee (#365)

(D) 1 ball, color light sea foam (#683)

dragonfly tote

Pack your bag and fly away with this delightful tote; it's a simple rectangle of half double crochet stitches. A discerning choice of colors and a whimsical dragonfly make it distinctive.

FINISHED MEASUREMENTS

11" wide x 15" high/28cm x 38cm excluding handle

YOU WILL NEED

325yd/297m of bulky weight yarn in green/brown multicolor (A)

30yd/27m of worsted weight yarn in fuchsia (B)

30yd/27m of worsted weight yarn in brown (C)

30yd/27m of worsted weight yarn in light green (D)

Hook: 5mm/H-8 or size needed to obtain gauge

Yarn needle

STITCHES USED

Chain (ch)

Double crochet (dc)

Half double crochet (hdc)

Single crochet (sc)

Slip stitch (sl st)

GAUGE

Take time to check your gauge.

12 hdc = 4"/10cm

9 rows = 4"/10cm

BAG

With A, ch 47.

Row 1: Hdc in 3rd ch from hook and in each ch across (45 hdc).

Row 2: Ch 2, turn, hdc in each hdc across.

Repeat Row 2 until piece measures about 23"/58 cm. Fasten off, leaving a 24"/61cm end for seaming.

HANDLE (MAKE 2)

With A, ch 7.

Row 1: Hdc in 3rd ch from hook and in each ch across (5 hdc).

Row 2: Ch 2, turn, hdc in each hdc across.

Repeat Row 2 until piece measures 26"/66cm. Fasten off, leaving a 12"/31cm end for sewing.

DRAGONFLY APPLIQUÉ

UPPER WINGS

With B, ch 14.

Row 1: Working in back bars of ch, sl st in first ch, sc in next ch, hdc in next ch, dc in next 8 ch, hdc in next ch, sc in next ch, sl st in last ch. Fasten off.

Rnd 2: Join C with sl st in first ch of Row 1, sc in each space between sts all the way around Row 1; join with sl st in first sc. Fasten off.

LOWER WINGS

With B, ch 12.

Row 1: Working in back bars of ch, sl st in first ch, sc in next ch, hdc in next ch, dc in next 6 ch, hdc in next ch, sc in next ch, sl st in last ch. Fasten off.

Rnd 2: Join C with sl st in first ch of Row 1, sc in each space between sts all the way around Row 1; join with sl st in first sc. Fasten off.

DRAGONFLY BODY

With D, ch 12.

Row 1: Working in back bars of ch, sl st in first ch, sc in next ch, hdc in next ch, dc in next 6 ch, hdc in next ch, sc in next ch, sl st in last ch, ch 4 for first antenna. Fasten off, leaving a 12"/31cm end for sewing.

Join D with sl st at base of first antenna, ch 4. Fasten off, leaving a 12"/31cm end for sewing.

FINISHING

Fold bag rectangle in half, bringing first row to meet last row. The sides of the bag are formed by the folded edge and where the first and last rows meet. Note lower right corner of bag. Unfold bag rectangle.

Using photograph as a guide, place upper and lower wings on lower right corner of the bag. With C, sew upper and lower wings in place. With D, sew dragonfly body across the wings. With yarn ends of the antennae, sew down antennae.

Fold bag rectangle in half, bringing first row to meet last row. With A, whipstitch the lower seam and side seam.

Whipstitch ends of first handle to front of bag 1½"/4cm in from each side edge. Take care not to twist handle when sewing second end. Repeat on back for second handle.

Weave in all yarn ends.

THIS PROJECT WAS CREATED WITH

Bernat's Soft Boucle, 97% acrylic, 3% polyester, 5oz/140g = 255yd/233m

(A) 2 balls, color teal twist (#26959)

Coats & Clark's Red Heart Super Saver (Economy) 100% acrylic, 7oz/198g = 364yd/333m

(B) 1 ball, color light fuchsia (#778)

(C) 1 ball, color cafe (#360)

(D) 1 ball, color light sage (#631)

blush blossom hair flower

FINISHED MEASUREMENTS

3½" diameter x 2½" deep/
  9cm x 6cm

YOU WILL NEED

40yd/37m worsted weight yarn in
  soft pink

Hook: 5.5mm/I-9 or size needed to
  obtain gauge

Yarn needle

Hair comb (available at most craft
  stores)

STITCHES USED

Chain (ch)

Double crochet (dc)

Slip stitch (sl st)

GAUGE

Take time to check your gauge.

First 2 rnds = 3½"/9cm

8 dc = 2"/5cm

This delicate crocheted flower exudes nonchalant beauty. Although there's a math property at work in its construction, you don't have to understand it to make this lovely ornament.

FLOWER

Ch 4; join with sl st in first ch to form a ring.

Rnd 1: Ch 3 (counts as first dc here and throughout), work 24 more dc in ring; join with sl st in top of beginning ch-3 (25 dc).

Rnd 2: Ch 3, 7 dc in same dc as join, work 8 dc in each dc around; join with sl st in top of beginning ch-3 (200 dc). Fasten off, leaving a 12"/31cm end for sewing.

FINISHING

Thread 24"/61cm end onto yarn needle and whipstitch back of flower to hair comb. Weave in all yarn ends.

THIS PROJECT WAS CREATED WITH

Coats & Clark's TLC Essentials, 100% acrylic, 6oz/170g = 312yd/285m, 1 ball of color light country rose (#2772)

little miss muff-it

FINISHED MEASUREMENTS
12" wide x 17" circumference/31cm x 43cm

YOU WILL NEED
250yd/229m of bulky weight yarn in dark pink (A)

50yd/46m of bulky weight boucle yarn in shades of grey (B)

Hook: 6mm/J-10 or size needed to obtain gauge

Yarn needle

STITCHES USED
Chain (ch)

Half double crochet (hdc)

Double crochet (dc)

Slip stitch (sl st)

GAUGE
Take time to check your gauge.

8 hdc = 4"/10cm

7 rows = 4"/10cm

Gloves are fine, but a soft and sophisticated muff is really something special. A thick, plush rectangle is worked with two strands of yarn held together, then formed into a cylinder and embellished with a double crochet ruffled border.

PATTERN NOTES
The body of the muff is worked with 2 strands of yarn held together.

Half double crochet stitches are worked in the spaces between stitches, not in the top of stitches. The last space is between the last stitch and the beginning chain of the previous row.

MUFF

With 2 strands of A held together, ch 27.

Row 1: Hdc in 3rd ch from hook and in each ch across (25 hdc).

Row 2: Ch 2, turn, hdc in each space between sts across (25 hdc).

Repeat Row 2 until piece measures 17"/43cm. Fasten off, leaving a 24"/61cm end for sewing.

RUFFLED EDGE (WORK TWICE)

Join B with sl st in corner of 1 long edge of muff.

Row 1: Working in ends of rows, ch 3, 2 dc in same st as join, 3 dc in end of each row across. Fasten off, leaving a 6"/15cm end for sewing.

Repeat ruffle on other long edge.

FINISHING

Using yarn end, sew last row of muff to first row to form a cylinder. Using yarn ends, sew ends of ruffle edges together. Weave in all yarn ends.

THIS PROJECT WAS CREATED WITH

Paton's Divine, 76.5% acrylic, 10.5% wool, 10.5% mohair, 2.5% polyester, 3.5oz/100g = 142yd/129m

(A) 2 balls, color richest rose (#06430)

Bernat's Soft Boucle, 97% acrylic, 3% polyester, 5oz/140g = 255yd/233m

(B) 1 ball, color grey shades (#26928)

flaming ribs

This scarf has rich deep ribs and fiery pompoms that demand to be noticed. Although the ribs may look difficult to make, all you have to do is work single crochet stitches in the back loops only.

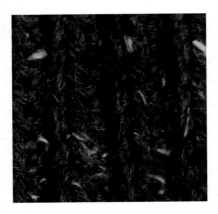

FINISHED MEASUREMENTS

6½" wide x 31" long/17cm x 79cm excluding pompoms

YOU WILL NEED

275yd/252m of worsted weight yarn in black tweed (A)

80yd/73m of worsted weight yarn in orange (B)

Hook: 4.5mm/G-7 or size needed to obtain gauge

Yarn needle

2½"/6cm pompom maker

STITCHES USED

Chain (ch)

Single crochet (sc)

GAUGE

Take time to check your gauge.

13 sc = 4"/10cm

12 rows = 4"/10cm

PATTERN NOTES

To create the rib stitch effect, the scarf is worked using single crochet stitches worked in the back loops only.

SCARF

With A, ch 103.

Row 1: Sc in 2nd ch from hook and in each ch across (102 sc).

Row 2: Ch 1, turn, working in back loops only, sc in each sc across.

Repeat Row 2 until piece measures 6½"/17cm. Fasten off.

FINISHING

POMPOM (MAKE 6)

With B, and your pompom maker, make 6 medium pompoms. With B, sew 1 pompom to each of the four corners of the scarf, and 1 pompom between the other 2 pompoms on each end.

Weave in all yarn ends.

THIS PROJECT WAS CREATED WITH

Caron's Simply Soft Tweed, 100% acrylic, 3oz/85g = 159yd/145m

(A) 2 balls, color black (#0010)

Coats & Clark's Red Heart Classic, 100% acrylic, 3.5oz/99g = 190yd/174m

(B) 1 ball, color tangerine (#253)

purse-sueded

Throw this tote over
your shoulder and
let the fringes fly.
The stitches worked
in luxurious suede yarn
produce a fascinating
interplay of light
and dark.

FINISHED MEASUREMENTS

8" wide x 9" tall + 6" fringe/20cm x 23cm + 15cm

YOU WILL NEED

350yd/320m of worsted weight suede ribbon yarn in medium green

Hook: 6mm/J-10 or size needed to obtain gauge

Yarn needle

6½" wide/17cm piece of heavy cardboard

STITCHES USED

Chain (ch)

Half double crochet (hdc)

Slip stitch (sl st)

GAUGE

Take time to check your gauge.

13 hdc = 4"/10cm

8 rows = 4"/10cm

PATTERN NOTES

The purse is worked with 2 strands of yarn held together. The shoulder strap is worked with a single strand of yarn.

PURSE

With 2 strands of yarn held together, ch 53.

Row 1: Hdc in 3rd ch from hook and in each ch across (51 hdc).

Rows 2–16: Ch 2, turn, hdc in each hdc across.

Fasten off and weave in all yarn ends.

UPPER EDGE

Hold piece to work along 1 short edge. With 2 strands of yarn held together, join yarn in corner of short edge.

Row 1: Ch 2, hdc in end of each row across.

Row 2: Ch 2, turn, hdc in each hdc across. Fasten off and weave in all yarn ends.

Repeat on opposite short edge.

SHOULDER STRAP

With 1 strand of yarn, ch 9.

Row 1: Hdc in 3rd ch from hook and in each ch across (7 hdc).

Row 2: Ch 2, turn, hdc in each hdc across.

Repeat Row 2 until strap measures 60"/152.4cm or desired length. Fasten off, leaving a 12"/30.5cm end for sewing.

FINISHING

Fold purse rectangle in half, upper edges together. Whipstitch side seams.

Sew ends of shoulder strap to upper edge of purse, centering ends of strap over side seams of purse. Ensure that strap is not twisted before sewing second shoulder strap end.

FRINGE

Wind yarn around 6½"/17cm piece of heavy cardboard 60 times. Cut along 1 end of wraps to create 60 strands, each about 13"/33cm long. Holding 3 strands together, fold strands in half. Using crochet hook, pull the folded end through a space at the lower edge of the purse. Use the crochet hook to pull the cut ends through the fold. Repeat this process across the lower edge to make 20 fringes. Trim the ends of the fringe to even.

Weave in all yarn ends.

THIS PROJECT WAS CREATED WITH

Berroco's Suede, 100% nylon, 1.75oz/50g = 120yd/111m, 2 balls of color maverick (#3716)

flapper gal

Feeling spunky? Wear this smart hat. Flapper Gal is worked in rounds from the top down.

SIZE

This hat is designed to fit most adult heads.

YOU WILL NEED

180yd/165m of worsted weight yarn in brown (A)

50yd/45m of worsted weight yarn in orange (B)

Hook: 4.5mm/G-7 or size needed to obtain gauge

Yarn needle

STITCHES USED

Chain (ch)

Half double crochet (hdc)

Single crochet (sc)

Slip stitch (sl st)

GAUGE

Take time to check your gauge.

First 5 rnds = 4"/10cm diameter

12 hdc = 4"/10cm

PATTERN NOTES

Half double crochet stitches are worked in the spaces between stitches, not in the top of stitches. The first space is between the beginning chain of the previous round and the next half double crochet.

HAT

With A, ch 2; join with sl st in first ch to form a ring.

Rnd 1: Ch 2 (counts as first hdc here and throughout), work 5 hdc in ring; join with sl st in top of beginning ch-2 (6 hdc).

Rnd 2: Ch 2, hdc in first space between sts, *2 hdc in next space between sts; repeat from * around; join with sl st in top of beginning ch-2 (12 hdc).

Rnd 3: Ch 2, hdc in first 2 spaces between sts, 2 hdc in next space between sts, *hdc in next space between sts, 2 hdc in next space between sts; repeat from * around to last space, skip last space; join with sl st in top of beginning ch-2 (17 hdc).

Rnd 4: Ch 2, hdc in first 3 spaces between sts, 2 hdc in next space between sts, *hdc in next 2 spaces between sts, 2 hdc in next space between sts; repeat from * around to last space, skip last space; join with sl st in top of beginning ch-2 (22 hdc).

Rnd 5: Ch 2, hdc in first 4 spaces between sts, 2 hdc in next space between sts, *hdc in next 3 spaces between sts, 2 hdc in next space between sts; repeat from * around to last space, skip last space; join with sl st in top of beginning ch-2 (27 hdc).

Rnd 6: Ch 2, hdc in first 5 spaces between sts, 2 hdc in next space between sts, *hdc in next 4 spaces between sts, 2 hdc in next space between sts; repeat from * around to last space, skip last space; join with sl st in top of beginning ch-2 (32 hdc).

Rnd 7: Ch 2, hdc in first 6 spaces between sts, 2 hdc in next space between sts, *hdc in next 5 spaces between sts, 2 hdc in next space between sts; repeat from * around to last space, skip last space; join with sl st in top of beginning ch-2 (37 hdc).

Rnds 8–12: Continue as established, working one more hdc between increases in each round (62 hdc).

Rnds 13–23: Ch 2, hdc in each space around; join with sl st in top of beginning ch-2.

Fasten off.

FIRST EARFLAP

With right side of the hat facing you, skip the first 8 spaces following the join, join A with sl st in next space.

Row 1: Ch 2 (counts as first hdc here and throughout), hdc in next 9 spaces between sts (10 hdc).

Rows 2–9: Ch 2, turn, hdc in each space across.

Fasten off.

SECOND EARFLAP

With wrong side of the hat facing you, skip the first 8 spaces following the join, join A with sl st in next space.

Row 1: Ch 2 (counts as first hdc here and throughout), hdc in next 9 spaces between sts (10 hdc).

Rows 2–9: Ch 2, turn, hdc in each space across.

Fasten off.

BORDER

With wrong side of the hat facing you, join B with sl st in back center space.

Rnd 1: Ch 1, work sc in each space around entire hat, working 2 sc in corners of earflaps; join with sl st in first sc. Fasten off.

FINISHING

Weave in all yarn ends.

THIS PROJECT WAS CREATED WITH

Paton's Décor, 75% acrylic, 25% wool, 3.5oz/100g = 210yd/193m

(A) 1 ball, color chocolate taupe (#01633)

Paton's Décor, 75% acrylic, 25% wool, 3.5oz/100g = 210yd/193m

(B) 1 ball, color burnt orange (#16605)

fluffster

Get your flirt on! Be warm *and* beautiful in this clever hat that's worked in rounds of half double crochet from the top down.

SIZE

This hat is designed to fit most adult heads.

YOU WILL NEED

180yd/165m of worsted weight mohair yarn in red/purple/orange multicolor

Hook: 4.5mm/G-7 or size needed to obtain gauge

Yarn needle

STITCHES USED

Chain (ch)

Double crochet (dc)

Half double crochet (hdc)

Slip stitch (sl st)

GAUGE

Take time to check your gauge.

First 6 rnds = 4"/10cm diameter

12 hdc = 4"/10cm

PATTERN NOTES

Half double crochet stitches are worked in the spaces between stitches, not in the tops of stitches. The first space is between the beginning chain of the previous round and the next half double crochet.

HAT

Ch 3; join with sl st in first ch to form a ring.

Rnd 1: Ch 2 (counts as first hdc here and throughout), work 5 hdc in ring; join with sl st in top of beginning ch-2 (6 hdc).

Rnd 2: Ch 2, hdc in first space between sts, *2 hdc in next space between sts; repeat from * around; join with sl st in top of beginning ch-2 (12 hdc).

Rnd 3: Ch 2, hdc in first 2 spaces between sts, 2 hdc in next space between sts, *hdc in next space between sts, 2 hdc in next space between sts; repeat from * around to last space, skip last space; join with sl st in top of beginning ch-2 (17 hdc).

Rnd 4: Ch 2, hdc in first 3 spaces between sts, 2 hdc in next space between sts, *hdc in next 2 spaces between sts, 2 hdc in next space between sts; repeat from * around to last space, skip last space; join with sl st in top of beginning ch-2 (22 hdc).

Rnd 5: Ch 2, hdc in first 4 spaces between sts, 2 hdc in next space between sts, *hdc in next 3 spaces between sts, 2 hdc in next space between sts; repeat from * around to last space, skip last space; join with sl st in top of beginning ch-2 (27 hdc).

Rnd 6: Ch 2, hdc in first 5 spaces between sts, 2 hdc in next space between sts, *hdc in next 4 spaces between sts, 2 hdc in next space between sts; repeat from * around to last space, skip last space; join with sl st in top of beginning ch-2 (32 hdc).

Rnd 7: Ch 2, hdc in first 6 spaces between sts, 2 hdc in next space between sts, *hdc in next 5 spaces between sts, 2 hdc in next space between sts; repeat from * around to last space, skip last space; join with sl st in top of beginning ch-2 (37 hdc).

Rnds 8–12: Continue as established, working one more hdc between increases in each round (62 hdc).

Rnds 13–27: Ch 2, hdc in each space around; join with sl st in top of beginning ch-2.

Row 28: Ch 1, sc in each space around; join with sl st in first sc. Fasten off.

FIRST EARFLAP

With right side of the hat facing you, skip the first 8 spaces following the join, join yarn with sl st in next space.

Row 1: Ch 2 (counts as first hdc here and throughout), hdc in next 8 spaces between sts (9 hdc).

Rows 2–27: Ch 2, turn, hdc in each space across.

Row 28: Ch 3 (counts as first dc here and throughout), dc in first st, (2 dc in next st) across (18 dc).

Row 29: Repeat Row 28 (36 dc). Fasten off.

SECOND EARFLAP

With wrong side of the hat facing you, skip the first 8 spaces following the join, join yarn with sl st in next space.

Row 1: Ch 2 (counts as first hdc here and throughout), hdc in next 8 spaces between sts (9 hdc).

Rows 2–29: Repeat Rows 2–29 of first earflap.

Fasten off.

FINISHING

Weave in all yarn ends.

THIS PROJECT WAS CREATED WITH

S.R. Kertzer's Knit 1, Purl 2 Sublime, 78% mohair, 13% wool, 9% nylon, 1.75oz/50g = 109yd/100m, 2 balls of color calypso sunset (#4006)

ewe fringe me

Indulge yourself in this incredible fringe. A striking texture enhances the drama of the fringes and is easily achieved by working crossed double crochet stitches.

FINISHED MEASUREMENTS

5" wide x 40" long + 16" fringe/
13cm x 102cm + 41cm

YOU WILL NEED

280yd/256m of bulky weight yarn
in medium green

Hook: 6.5mm/K-10.5 or size needed to obtain gauge

16½"/42cm piece of heavy cardboard

Yarn needle

STITCHES USED

Chain (ch)

Half double crochet (hdc)

Double crochet (dc)

Crossed double crochet (cdc): Skip
next st, dc in next st; working
around dc just made, dc in
skipped st.

GAUGE

Take time to check your gauge.

10 dc = 4"/10cm

4½ rows = 4"/10cm

SCARF

Ch 15.

Row 1: Hdc in 3rd ch from hook and in each ch across (13 hdc).

Row 2: Ch 3 (counts as first dc here and throughout), turn, *skip next st, dc in next st; working around dc just made, dc in skipped st (cdc made), dc in next st; repeat from * across.

Row 3: Ch 3, turn, dc in each dc across.

Repeat Rows 2 and 3 until piece measures 40"/102cm. Do not fasten off.

Last Row: Ch 2, turn, hdc in each st across. Fasten off.

FINISHING

Weave in all yarn ends.

FRINGE

Wind yarn around 16½"/42cm piece of heavy cardboard 120 times. Cut along 1 end of wraps to create 120 strands each about 33"/84cm long. Holding 5 strands together, fold strands in half. Using crochet hook, pull the folded end through the space between the first 2 stitches of the last row. Use the crochet hook to pull the cut ends through the fold. Repeat this process across the row, then turn scarf and attach fringe in the same manner along the opposite end. Trim the ends of the fringe to even.

THIS PROJECT WAS CREATED WITH

Brown Sheep Company's Lamb's Pride Bulky Weight, 85% wool, 15% mohair, 3.5oz/99g = 125yd/114m, 3 balls of color kiwi (#M191)

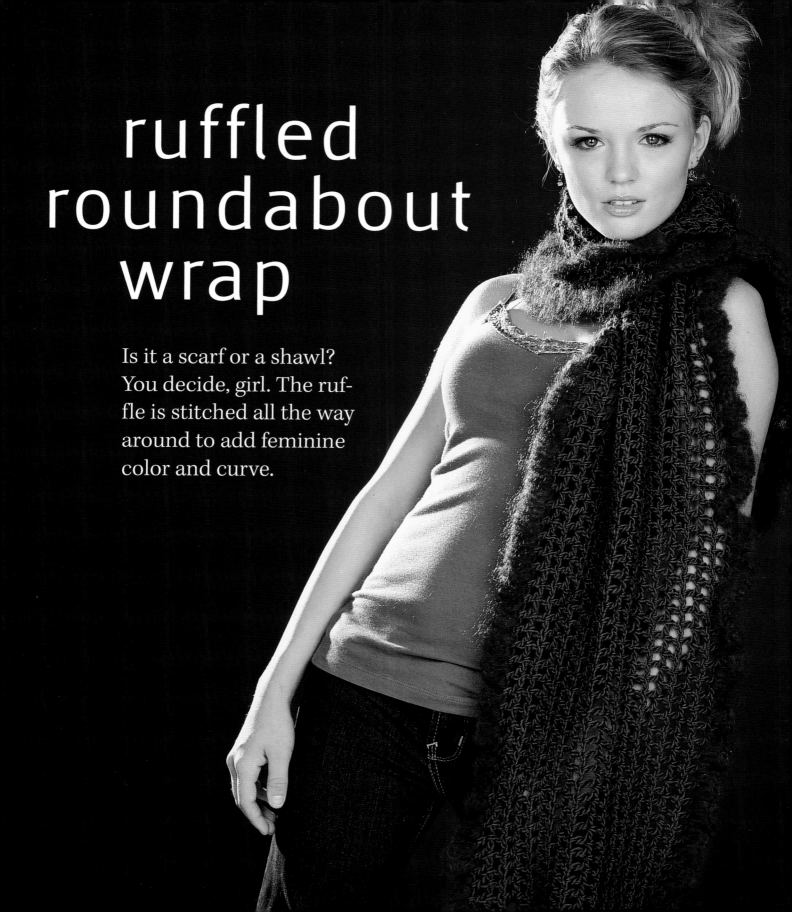

ruffled roundabout wrap

Is it a scarf or a shawl? You decide, girl. The ruffle is stitched all the way around to add feminine color and curve.

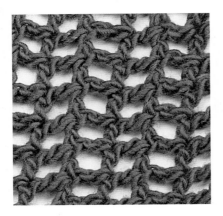

FINISHED MEASUREMENTS
13" wide x 60" long/33cm x 152cm

YOU WILL NEED
300yd/274m of worsted weight yarn in green (A)

250yd/229m of sport weight yarn in burgundy (B)

Hook: 6mm/J-10 or size needed to obtain gauge

Yarn needle

STITCHES USED
Chain (ch)

Double crochet (dc)

Half double crochet (hdc)

Slip stitch (sl st)

GAUGE
Take time to check your gauge.

7 (dc, ch 1) repeats = 4"/10cm

6 rows = 4"/10cm

WRAP
With A, ch 213.

Row 1: Hdc in 3rd ch from hook and in each ch across (211 hdc).

Row 2: Ch 4 (counts as first dc, ch 1 here and throughout), turn, skip next hdc, dc in next hdc, *ch 1, skip next hdc, dc in next hdc; repeat from * across.

Rows 3–17: Ch 4, turn, skip next ch-1 space, dc in next dc, *ch 1, skip next ch-1 space, dc in next dc; repeat from * across.

Row 18: Ch 2 (counts as first hdc), turn, hdc in each dc and ch-1 space across. Fasten off.

RUFFLE
Join B with sl st in first ch on opposite side of foundation chain.

Rnd 1: Ch 3 (counts as first dc here and throughout), 5 dc in same st as join (corner made); working along opposite side of foundation chain, *skip 1 ch, 3 dc in next ch; repeat from * across to last ch, 6 dc in last ch (corner made); turn to work in ends of rows along short edge, 3 dc in end of each row across; turn to work across last row, 6 dc in first st (corner made), *skip 1 st, 3 dc in next st; repeat from * across to last st, 6 dc in last st (corner made); turn to work in ends of rows along short edge, 3 dc in end of each row across; join with sl st in top of beginning ch-3. Fasten off.

FINISHING
Weave in all yarn ends.

THIS PROJECT WAS CREATED WITH

Brown Sheep Company's Lamb's Pride Worsted Weight, 85% wool, 15% mohair, 3.5oz/99g = 190yd/174m

(A) 3 balls, color turkish olive (#M41)

GGH's Soft-Kid, 70% super kid mohair, 25% nylon, 5% wool, 0.88oz/25g = 151yd/138m

(B) 2 balls, color color #37

medallion clutch

A stylish handbag is a girl's best friend. Half double crochet stitches form the body of the clutch, while the medallion is made of increasing rounds of single crochet.

FINISHED MEASUREMENTS
14" wide x 7" tall/36cm x 18cm

YOU WILL NEED
190yd/174m of worsted weight
   yarn in medium blue (A)

190yd/174m of worsted weight
   yarn in lavender (B)

45yd/41m of worsted weight
   ribbon yarn in copper (C)

20yd/18m of worsted weight
   ribbon yarn in gold/black
   metallic (D)

Hook: 6mm/J-10 or size needed to
   obtain gauge

Yarn needle

Sewing needle and matching
   thread (for attaching snap
   closure)

¾"/18mm snap closure

1yd/.9m square of felt (optional)

STITCHES USED
Chain (ch)

Half double crochet (hdc)

Double crochet (dc)

Single crochet (sc)

Slip stitch (sl st)

GAUGE
Take time to check your gauge.

10 hdc = 4"/10cm

9 rows = 4"/10cm

PATTERN NOTES
Half double crochet stitches are worked in the spaces between stitches, not in the top of stitches. The last space is between the last stitch and the beginning chain of the previous row.

The clutch is worked holding 1 strand each of 2 different colors of yarn together.

The medallion is worked holding 2 strands of ribbon yarn together.

Lining this clutch is optional because the stitches are worked close together.

CLUTCH

With 1 strand each of A and B held together, ch 40.

Row 1: Hdc in 3rd ch from hook and in each ch across (38 hdc).

Row 2: Ch 2, turn, hdc in each space between sts across (38 hdc).

Repeat Row 2 until piece measures 14"/36cm. Fasten off and weave in all yarn ends.

MEDALLION CLOSURE

With 2 strands of C held together, ch 3; join with sl st in first ch to form a ring.

Rnd 1: Ch 1 (counts as first sc here and throughout), work 8 more sc in ring; join with sl st in beginning ch-1 (9 sc).

Rnd 2: Ch 1, sc in same st as join, 2 sc in each sc around; join with sl st in beginning ch-1 (18 sc).

Rnd 3: Ch 1, sc in same st as join, sc in next sc, *2 sc in next sc, sc in next sc; repeat from * around; join with sl st in beginning ch-1 (27 sc). Fasten off and weave in all ends.

Rnd 4: Join D with a sl st in any st of Rnd 3, ch 1 (counts as first sc), sc in same st as join, *2 sc in next sc, sc in next sc; repeat from * around; join with sl st in beginning ch-1 (41 sc). Fasten off and weave in all ends.

FINISHING

LINE CLUTCH

Lay clutch rectangle on top of felt on a flat surface. Trace around rectangle. Remove clutch, measure 1"/3cm in from one short edge and 1"/3cm in from one long edge, and cut out rectangle of felt.

Lay felt rectangle centered on top of clutch rectangle. There should be about ½"/1cm of clutch extending past all the edges of the felt rectangle.

Whipstitch edges of felt lining to clutch. Make sure the stitches do not show on the front of the clutch.

FORM POCKET OF CLUTCH

Fold one short edge of clutch rectangle about 4½"/11cm up over lining.

Whipstitch side seams together.

Weave in all yarn ends.

Center medallion over front flap of clutch. Whipstitch medallion in place. Sew snap closure to back of half of medallion that extends over front flap. Sew other half of snap closure centered about 1"/3cm above lower edge of clutch.

THIS PROJECT WAS CREATED WITH

Coats & Clark's Red Heart Classic, 100% acrylic, 3.5oz/99g = 190yd/174m

(A) 1 ball, color blue jewel (#818)

(B) 1 ball, color light lavender (#579)

Colinette's Giotto, 50% cotton, 40% rayon, 10% nylon, 3.5oz/100g = 156yd/143m

(C) 1 ball, color red parrot (#15)

Berroco's Metallic FX , 85% rayon, 15% metallic, 0.88oz/25g = 85yd/78m

(D) 1 ball, color gold/black (#1003)

chapeau l'orange

SIZE

This hat is designed to fit most adult heads.

YOU WILL NEED

100yd/91m of super bulky weight yarn in orange-multicolor

Hook: 10mm/N-15 or size needed to obtain gauge

Yarn needle

STITCHES USED

Chain (ch)

Double crochet (dc)

Slip stitch (sl st)

GAUGE

Take time to check your gauge.

First 3 rnds = 4"/10cm

10 dc = 4"/10cm

If you believe redheads have more fun, don this cap and see for yourself. This hat is worked in the round from the top down and finished with a nifty wraparound earflap.

PATTERN NOTES

Double crochet stitches are worked in the spaces between stitches, not in the tops of stitches. The first space is between the beginning chain of the previous round and the next double crochet.

HAT

Ch 3; join with sl st in first ch to form a ring.

Rnd 1: Ch 3 (counts as first dc here and throughout), work 6 dc in ring; join with sl st in top of beginning ch-3 (7 dc).

Rnd 2: Ch 3, dc in first space between sts, *2 dc in next space between sts; repeat from * around; join with sl st in top of beginning ch-3 (14 dc).

Rnd 3: Ch 3, dc in first 2 spaces between sts, *2 dc in next space between sts, dc in next space between sts; repeat from * around; join with sl st in top of beginning ch-3 (21 dc).

Rnd 4: Ch 3, dc in first 3 spaces between sts, *2 dc in next space between sts, dc in next 2 spaces between sts; repeat from * around; join with sl st in top of beginning ch-3 (28 dc).

Rnd 5: Ch 3, dc in first 4 spaces between sts, *2 dc in next space between sts, dc in next 3 spaces between sts; repeat from * around; join with sl st in top of beginning ch-3 (35 dc).

Rnd 6: Ch 3, dc in first 5 spaces between sts, *2 dc in next space between sts, dc in next 4 spaces between sts; repeat from * around; join with sl st in top of beginning ch-3 (42 dc).

Rnd 7: Ch 3, dc in first 6 spaces between sts, *2 dc in next space between sts, dc in next 5 spaces between sts; repeat from * around; join with sl st in top of beginning ch-3 (49 dc).

Rnds 8–11: Ch 3, dc in each space between sts around; join with sl st in top of beginning ch-3.

Fasten off.

WRAPAROUND EARFLAP

With the wrong side of the hat facing you, skip the first 13 spaces following the join, join yarn with sl st in the next space.

Row 1: Ch 3 (counts as first dc here and throughout), turn, dc in next 27 spaces between sts (28 dc).

Rows 2–3: Ch 3, turn, dc in each space across.

Fasten off.

FINISHING

Weave in all yarn ends.

THIS PROJECT WAS CREATED WITH

Coats & Clark's Red Heart Light & Lofty, 100% acrylic, 4.5oz/127g = 105yd/96m, 1 ball of color paprika multi (#9930)

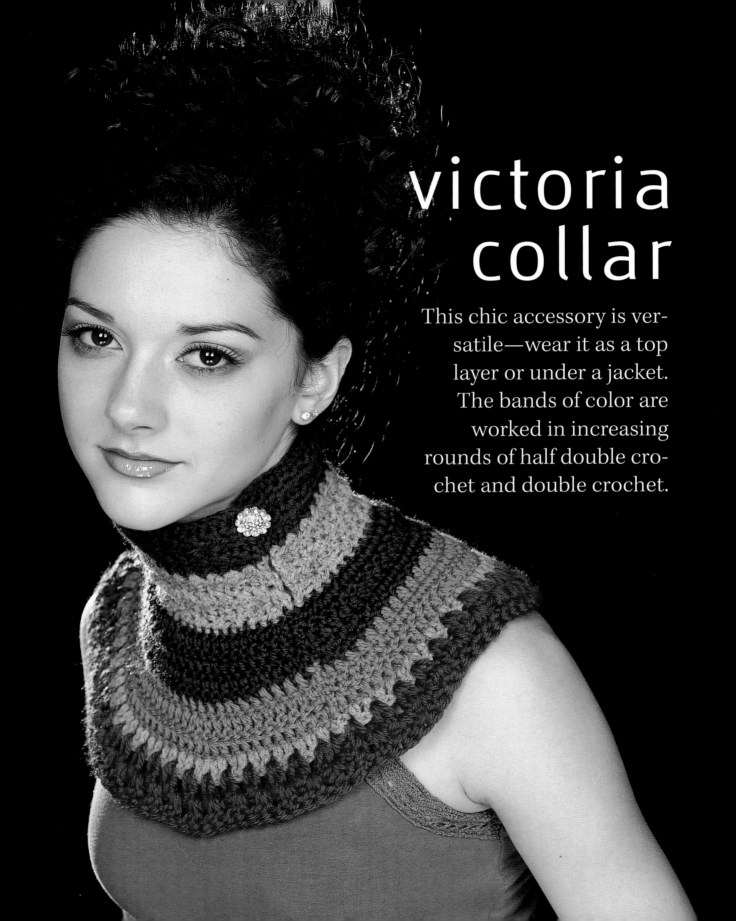

victoria collar

This chic accessory is versatile—wear it as a top layer or under a jacket. The bands of color are worked in increasing rounds of half double crochet and double crochet.

FINISHED MEASUREMENTS

8½" long x 15" upper circumference x 32" lower circumference/22cm x 38.1cm x 81.3cm

YOU WILL NEED

35yd/32m of worsted weight yarn in medium blue (A)

35yd/32m of worsted weight yarn in camel (B)

40yd/37m of worsted weight yarn in purple (C)

40yd/37m of worsted weight yarn in green (D)

50yd/46m of worsted weight yarn in light pink (E)

50yd/46m of worsted weight yarn in fuchsia (F)

Hooks: 6.5mm/K-10.5 and 6mm/J-10 or size needed to obtain gauge

Yarn needle

Button, 1"/3cm diameter

STITCHES USED

Chain (ch)

Double crochet (dc)

Half double crochet (hdc)

Single crochet (sc)

Slip stitch (sl st)

GAUGE

Take time to check your gauge.

16 hdc = 4"/10cm with smaller hook

9 rows = 4"/10cm with smaller hook

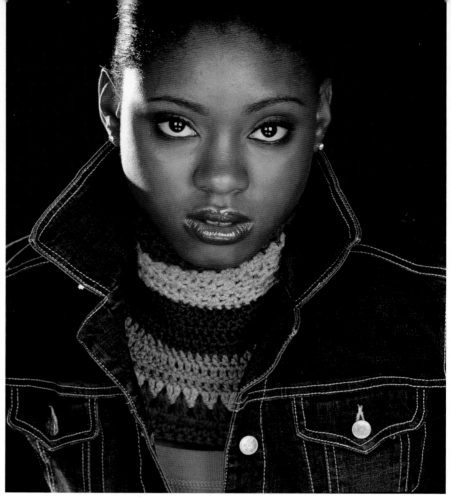

PATTERN NOTE

To change color, work last stitch to the last yarn over, yarn over with the new color, and draw through all loops on hook to complete the stitch. Fasten off old color.

COLLAR

Beginning at top of neck, with smaller hook and A, ch 60.

Row 1: Hdc in 3rd ch from hook (skipped ch-2 counts as first hdc) and in each ch across (59 hdc).

Rows 2–5: Ch 2 (counts as first hdc here and throughout), turn, skip next hdc, *2 hdc in next hdc, skip next hdc; repeat from * across to last hdc, hdc in last hdc; change to B in last st of last row.

Rows 6–10: Repeat Row 2; change to C in last st of last row.

Note: Work is now joined into a ring and progresses in rounds.

Rnd 11: Ch 2, hdc in same st (1 st increased), hdc in each st around; join with sl st in top of beginning ch-2 (60 hdc).

Rnd 12: Ch 3 (counts as first dc here and throughout), dc in next 9 sts, 2 dc in next st, *dc in next 10 sts, 2 dc in next st; repeat from * around to last 5 sts, dc in last 5 sts; join with sl st in top of beginning ch-3 (65 sts).

Rnd 13: Ch 3, dc in same st as join (1 st increased), *dc in next 10 sts, 2 dc in next st; repeat from * around to last 9 sts, dc in last 9 sts; join with sl st in top of beginning ch-3 (71 sts).

Rnd 14: Ch 3, dc in next 9 sts, 2 dc in next st, *dc in next 10 sts, 2 dc in next st; repeat from * around to last 5 sts, dc in last 5 sts; join with sl st in top of beginning ch-3 (77 sts); change to D in last st.

Rnd 15: Ch 3, dc in same st as join, *dc in next 10 sts, 2 dc in next st; repeat from * around to last 10 sts, dc in last 10 sts; join with sl st in top of beginning ch-3 (84 sts).

Rnd 16: Ch 3, dc in next 9 sts, 2 dc in next st, *dc in next 10 sts, 2 dc in next st; repeat from * around to last 7 sts, dc in last 7 sts; join with sl st in top of beginning ch-3 (91 sts).

Rnd 17: Ch 3, dc in same st as join, *dc in next 10 sts, 2 dc in next st; repeat from * around to last 2 sts, dc in last 2 sts; join with sl st in top of beginning ch-3 (100 sts); change to E in last st.

Rnd 18: Ch 3, dc in next 9 sts, 2 dc in next st, *dc in next 10 sts, 2 dc in next st; repeat from * around to last st, dc in last st; join with sl st in top of beginning ch-3 (109 sts); change to larger hook and F in last st.

Rnd 19: Ch 3, dc in first space between sts, *ch 1, skip next space between sts, 2 dc in next space between sts; repeat from * around; join with sl st in top of beginning ch-3 (110 sts).

Rnd 20: Ch 3, 2 dc in each ch-1 space around; join with sl st in top of beginning ch-3. Fasten off, leaving a 12"/31cm end for sewing.

FINISHING

BUTTON LOOP

With right side facing, join A with sl st in right edge of Row 1, ch 4, sl st in right edge of Row 3. Fasten off and securely weave in ends.

Sew button to top left neck edge opening opposite button loop.

Weave in all yarn ends.

THIS PROJECT WAS CREATED WITH

Lion Brand's Wool-Ease Worsted Weight, 80% acrylic, 20% wool, 3oz/85g = 197yd/180m

(A) 1 ball, color blue mist (#115)

(B) 1 ball, color camel (#125)

(C) 1 ball, color plum (#145)

(D) 1 ball, color forest green heather (#180)

(E) 1 ball, color rose heather (#140)

Coats & Clark's Red Heart Soft, 100% acrylic, 5oz/140g = 256yd/234m

(F) 1 ball, color fuschia (#9537)

jardin scarf

FINISHED MEASUREMENTS

7" wide x 40" long/18cm x 102cm

YOU WILL NEED

220yd/201m of worsted weight yarn in green/blue multicolor (A)

35yd/32m of worsted weight yarn in brown (B)

35yd/32m of worsted weight yarn in pink (C)

35yd/32m of worsted weight yarn in purple (D)

35yd/32m of worsted weight yarn in orange (E)

35yd/32m of worsted weight yarn in dark purple (F)

35yd/32m of worsted weight yarn in light green (G)

35yd/32m of worsted weight yarn in dark brown (H)

Hook: 5mm/H-8 or size needed to obtain gauge

Yarn needle

STITCHES USED

Chain (ch)

Half double crochet (hdc)

Double crochet (dc)

Slip stitch (sl st)

GAUGE

Take time to check your gauge.

12 dc = 4"/10cm

8 rows = 4"/10cm

Banish the winter blahs when you sport this brightly colored floral scarf; it's worked in crossed stitches to create a texture suggestive of a green garden.

SCARF

With A, ch 20.

Row 1: Hdc in 3rd ch from hook and in each ch across (18 hdc).

Row 2: Ch 3 (counts as first dc here and throughout), turn, *skip next st, dc in next st; working around dc just made, dc in skipped st (crossed dc made); repeat from * across to last st, dc in last st.

Row 3: Ch 2, turn, hdc in each dc across.

Repeat Rows 2 and 3 until piece is 39"/99cm long. Do not fasten off.

Border Rnd: Ch 3, turn, 3 dc in first st, dc in each st across to last st, 4 dc in last st (corner made); pivot scarf to work in ends of rows along long edge of scarf, work dc evenly spaced along long edge; pivot scarf to work in free loops of foundation ch, 4 dc in first ch, dc in each ch across to last ch, 4 dc in last ch; pivot scarf to work in ends of rows along other long edge of scarf, work dc evenly spaced along long edge; join with sl st in top of beginning ch-3. Fasten off.

FLOWER #1

With B, ch 4; join with sl st in first ch to form a ring.

Rnd 1: Ch 3 (counts as first dc), work 11 more dc in ring; join with sl st in top of beginning ch-3 (12 dc). Fasten off.

Rnd 2: Join C with sl st in any space between sts, ch 6, *sl st in next space between sts, ch 6; repeat from * around; join with sl st in first sl st (12 ch-6 petals). Fasten off, leaving a 12"/31cm end for sewing.

FLOWER #2

With D, ch 4; join with sl st in first ch to form a ring.

Rnd 1: Ch 2 (counts as first hdc), work 8 more hdc in ring; join with sl st in top of beginning ch-2 (9 hdc). Fasten off.

Rnd 2: Join E with sl st in any space between sts, ch 2, *sl st in next space between sts, ch 2; repeat from * around; join with sl st in first sl st (9 ch-2 spaces).

Rnd 3: (Sl st, hdc, dc, hdc, sl st) in each ch-2 space around (9 petals). Fasten off, leaving a 12"/31cm end for sewing.

FLOWER #3

With H, ch 4; join with sl st in first ch to form a ring.

Rnd 1: Ch 2 (counts as first hdc), work 7 more hdc in ring; join with sl st in top of beginning ch-2 (8 hdc). Fasten off.

Rnd 2: Join G with sl st in any space between sts, ch 2, *sl st in next space between sts, ch 2; repeat from * around; join with sl st in first sl st (8 ch-2 spaces).

Rnd 3: (Sc, hdc, dc, hdc, sc) in each ch-2 space around (8 petals). Fasten off.

Rnd 4: Join F with sl st around any st of Rnd 3, sl st around each st around. Fasten off, leaving a 12"/31cm end for sewing.

FINISHING

Using photograph as a guide, sew flowers to one end of scarf. Weave in all yarn ends.

THIS PROJECT WAS CREATED WITH

Bernat's Berella Ombre, 100% acrylic, 3oz/85g = 165yd/150m

(A) 2 balls, color seascape ombre (#2160)

Karabella's Aurora 8, 100% extra fine merino, 1.75oz/50g = 98yd/90m

(B) 1 ball, color #258

(C) 1 ball, color #47

(D) 1 ball, color #803

(E) 1 ball, color #8

(F) 1 ball, color #2

(G) 1 ball, color #82

(H) 1 ball, color #49

pompom scarf

Unexpected red pompoms take the striped scarf from traditional to au courant. Working half double crochets in the spaces between stitches gives this scarf a sturdy texture, greater thickness, and lots of warmth.

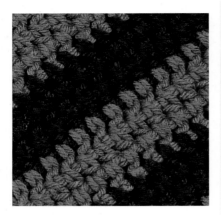

FINISHED MEASUREMENTS

6" wide x 34" long/15cm x 86cm

YOU WILL NEED

120yd/110m of worsted weight yarn in dark green (A)

100yd/91m of worsted weight yarn in light purple (B)

80yd/73m of worsted weight yarn in red (C)

Hook: 5.5mm/I-9 or size needed to obtain gauge

Yarn needle

2½"/6cm pompom maker

STITCHES USED

Chain (ch)

Half double crochet (hdc)

GAUGE

Take time to check your gauge.

11 hdc = 4"/10cm

9½ rows = 4"/10cm

PATTERN NOTES

Half double crochet stitches are worked in the spaces between stitches, not in the tops of stitches. The last space is between the last stitch and the beginning chain of the previous row.

To change color, work last stitch to the last yarn over, yarn over with the new color, and draw through all loops on hook to complete the stitch. Fasten off old color.

SCARF

With A, ch 18.

Row 1: Hdc in 3rd ch from hook and in each ch across (16 hdc).

Rows 2–3: Ch 2, turn, hdc in each space between sts across (16 hdc); change to B in last st of last row.

Rows 4–6: Repeat Row 2; change to A in last st of last row.

Rows 7–9: Repeat Row 2.

Rows 10–15: Repeat Rows 4–9; change to B in last st of last row.

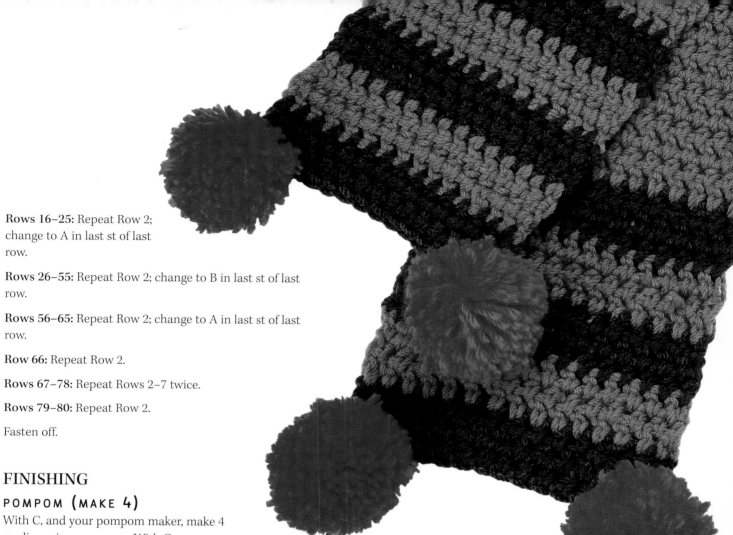

Rows 16–25: Repeat Row 2; change to A in last st of last row.

Rows 26–55: Repeat Row 2; change to B in last st of last row.

Rows 56–65: Repeat Row 2; change to A in last st of last row.

Row 66: Repeat Row 2.

Rows 67–78: Repeat Rows 2–7 twice.

Rows 79–80: Repeat Row 2.

Fasten off.

FINISHING
POMPOM (MAKE 4)

With C, and your pompom maker, make 4 medium-size pompoms. With C, sew one pompom to each of the four corners of the scarf.

Weave in all yarn ends.

THIS PROJECT WAS CREATED WITH

Coats & Clark's TLC Essentials, 100% acrylic, 6oz/170g = 312yd/285m

(A) 1 ball, color dark thyme (#2675)

(B) 1 ball, color light plum (#2531)

Caron's Simply Soft Brites, 100% acrylic, 6oz/170g = 330yd/302m

(C) 1 ball, color watermelon (#9604)

two-toned tote

FINISHED MEASUREMENTS

11" wide x 12" high/28cm x 31cm
excluding handle

YOU WILL NEED

300yd/274m of worsted weight yarn
in blue/green (A)

150yd/137m of worsted weight yarn
in brown (B)

100yd/91m of worsted weight
metallic yarn in gold (C)

Hook: 6mm/J-10 or size needed to
obtain gauge

Yarn needle

1yd/.9m square of felt in brown
(optional)

2 plastic hoop handles, 5½"/14cm
diameter

STITCHES USED

Chain (ch)

Double crochet (dc)

Half double crochet (hdc)

Slip stitch (sl st)

GAUGE

Take time to check your gauge.

16 hdc = 4"/10cm

10 rows = 4"/10cm

Every fashionista needs a tote with bling.
The gold metallic flower complements the
intriguing texture that's quickly achieved with
groupings of half double crochet stitches.

PATTERN NOTE

To change color, work last stitch to the last yarn over, yarn over with the new
color, and draw through all loops on hook to complete the stitch. Fasten off old
color.

BAG

With A, ch 114.

Row 1: Hdc in 3rd ch from hook and in each ch across (112 hdc).

Row 2: Ch 2, turn, hdc in first st, *skip next st, 2 hdc in next st; repeat from *
across to last st, hdc in last st.

Rows 3–9: Repeat Row 2.

Row 10: Repeat Row 2; change to B in last st of last row.

Rows 11–17: Repeat Row 2.

Row 18: Repeat Row 2; change to A in last st of last row.

Rows 19–28: Repeat Row 2.

Fasten off.

FLOWER

With C, ch 4; join with sl st in first ch to form a ring.

Rnd 1: Ch 4 (counts as first dc, ch 1), *dc in ring, ch 1; repeat from * 8 more times; join with sl st in 3rd ch of beginning ch-4 (10 ch-1 spaces).

Rnd 2: Ch 3, work 5 dc in first ch-1 space, *6 dc in next ch-1 space; repeat from * around; join with sl st in top of beginning ch-3 (60 dc). Fasten off.

With right side facing and working behind Rnd 2 stitches, join C with a sl st in any ch-1 space of Rnd 1.

Rnd 3: Ch 6 (counts as first dc, ch 3), dc in next ch-1 space of Rnd 1, *ch 3, dc in next ch-1 space of Rnd 1; repeat from * around; ch 3; join with sl st in 3rd ch of beginning ch-6 (10 ch-3 spaces).

Rnd 4: Ch 3, 7 dc in first ch-3 space, *8 dc in next ch-3 space; repeat from * around; join with sl st in 3rd ch of beginning ch-3. Fasten off, leaving a 12"/31cm end for sewing.

FINISHING

LINE TOTE (OPTIONAL)

Lay tote rectangle on top of felt on a flat surface. Trace around rectangle. Remove rectangle, measure 5"/13cm in from each short edge and ½"/1cm in from each long edge, and cut out rectangle of felt.

Lay felt rectangle centered on top of tote rectangle. About 5"/13cm of the tote rectangle should extend past the short edges and ½"/1cm should extend past the long edges of the felt rectangle.

Whipstitch edges of felt lining to tote rectangle. Make sure the stitches do not show on the front of the tote rectangle.

Fold tote rectangle in half, bringing short edges together at the top. Leaving upper 5"/13cm open, whipstitch side seams together.

Using photograph as a guide, sew flower to upper-right corner of front of bag.

Fold and gather upper edge of 1 side of bag over 1 handle and sew upper edge to inside of bag to secure handle. Repeat to attach second handle to other side of bag.

Weave in all yarn ends.

THIS PROJECT WAS CREATED WITH

*Coats & Clark's Red Heart Super Saver (Economy), 100%
    acrylic, 7oz/198g = 364yd/333m*

(A) 1 ball, color dusty teal (#657)

*Coats & Clark's Red Heart Super Saver, 100% acrylic, 3oz/85g
    = 160yd/146m*

(B) 1 ball, color brown (#328)

*GGH's Rebecca Gold Lamé, 62% rayon, 38% polyester,
    0.88oz/25g = 210yd/192m*

(C) 1 ball, color gold (#100)

pretty in pink

FINISHED MEASUREMENTS
5" wide x 30" long/13cm x 76cm

YOU WILL NEED
175yd/160m of fine weight yarn in medium pink

Hook: 5.5mm/I-9 or size needed to obtain gauge

Yarn needle

STITCHES USED
Chain (ch)

Half double crochet (hdc)

Double crochet (dc)

Slip stitch (sl st)

GAUGE
Take time to check your gauge.

11 dc = 4"/10cm

5 rows = 4"/10cm

Here's a versatile, on-trend scarf: you can drape it loosely around your neck, use it as a lacey head wrap, or tie up your ponytail. This scarf is a joy to make in light, fluffy yarn.

PATTERN NOTES
Double crochet stitches are worked in the spaces between stitches, not in the tops of stitches. The last space is between the last stitch and the beginning chain of the previous row.

SCARF

Ch 15.

Row 1: Hdc in 3rd ch from hook and in each ch across (13 hdc).

Row 2: Ch 3 (counts as first dc here and throughout), turn, *skip next space between sts, 2 dc in next space between sts; repeat from * across to last space, skip last space, dc in top of beginning ch-2.

Rows 3–29: Ch 3, turn, *skip next space between sts, 2 dc in next space between sts; repeat from * across to last space, skip last space, dc in top of beginning ch-3.

Row 30: Ch 2, turn, hdc in each dc across (14 hdc). Do not fasten off.

RUFFLE (WORK TWICE)

Row 1: Ch 3, turn, 2 dc in first hdc, 3 dc in each hdc across (42 dc).

Row 2: Ch 3, turn, dc in first dc, 2 dc in each dc across (84 dc).

Row 3: Ch 3, turn, dc in first dc, 2 dc in each dc across (168 dc). Fasten off.

Join yarn with sl st in first ch on opposite side of foundation chain. Repeat Rows 1–3 to make ruffle on other end of scarf. Fasten off.

FINISHING

Weave in all yarn ends.

THIS PROJECT WAS CREATED WITH

Paton's Lacette, 39% nylon, 36% acrylic, 25% mohair, 1.75oz/50g = 235yd/215m, 1 ball of color maroon mist (#30405)

wrap star

Get your glam on with this
sensational lightweight wrap.
It's worked in increasing rows
of half double crochet from the
lower tip to wide top edge and
then embellished with dramatic
metallic fringe.

FINISHED MEASUREMENTS

29" wide x 45" long/74cm x 114cm
  excluding fringe

YOU WILL NEED

190yd/174m of sport weight yarn in
  black (A)

500yd/457m of sport weight metallic
  yarn in gold/black (B)

Hook: 5.5mm/I-9 or size needed to
  obtain gauge

Yarn needle

11" wide/28cm piece of heavy cardboard

STITCHES USED

Chain (ch)

Half double crochet (hdc)

GAUGE

Take time to check your gauge.

10 hdc = 4"/10cm

7 rows = 4"/10cm

WRAP

Beginning at lower tip of wrap with A, ch 5.

Row 1: 2 hdc in 4th ch from hook (skipped ch-3 counts as hdc, ch 1), ch 1, hdc in last ch (4 hdc).

Row 2: Ch 2, turn, hdc in space between first 2 sts, skip 2 center sts, 2 hdc in space between last hdc and beginning ch-4, hdc in 3rd ch of beginning ch-4.

Note: The last space in a row is the space between the last hdc and the beginning ch.

Row 3: Ch 2, turn, hdc in first space between sts, *skip 2 sts, 2 hdc in next space between sts; repeat across; hdc in top of beginning ch-2.

Repeat Row 3 until wrap is about 45"/114.3cm. Fasten off and weave in all ends.

FINISHING

FRINGE

Wind yarn around 11"/28cm piece of heavy cardboard. Cut along one end of wraps to create strands about 22"/56cm long. Holding 5 strands together, fold strands in half. Using crochet hook pull the folded end through the end of a row at the edge of the wrap. Use the crochet hook to pull the cut ends through the fold. Repeat this process, working fringe in the end of each row along the entire lower edge of the shawl. Attach a fringe to the lower tip of the shawl. Trim the ends of the fringe to even.

THIS PROJECT WAS CREATED WITH

Karabella's Aurora 8, 100% extra fine merino, 1.75oz/50g = 98yd/90m

(A) 2 balls, color #01

GGH's Lamé, 62% rayon, 38% polyester, 0.88oz/25g = 210yd/192m

(B) 3 balls, color gold/black #102

papillon scarf

This cozy scarf is the perfect size to tuck neatly around your neck and inside your coat, although you'll surely want to let the butterfly fly free. The appliqué is made with craft felt and sewn to the scarf.

FINISHED MEASUREMENTS
5" wide x 33" long/13cm x 84cm

YOU WILL NEED
105yd/96m of worsted weight yarn in orange

Hook: 6mm/J-10 or size needed to obtain gauge

Yarn needle

Black embroidery floss

Embroidering needle

4 sheets of craft felt; 1 each brown, light brown, red, and gold

Glue stick

STITCHES USED
Chain (ch)

Half double crochet (hdc)

Single crochet (sc)

GAUGE
Take time to check your gauge.

12 sts = 4"/10cm

10 rows = 4"/10cm

PATTERN NOTE
Half double crochet stitches are worked in the spaces between stitches, not in the tops of stitches. The last space is between the last stitch and the beginning chain of the previous row.

SCARF
Ch 18.

Row 1: Hdc in 3rd ch from hook and in each ch across (16 hdc).

Row 2: Ch 2, turn, hdc in first hdc, skip first space between sts, *2 hdc in next space between sts, skip next space between sts; repeat from * 6 more times, 2 hdc in last space between sts.

Repeat Row 2 until scarf measures about 33"/84cm long. Fasten off.

FINISHING

BUTTERFLY APPLIQUÉ

Trace butterfly template (at right) and use as a guide to cut parts of butterfly from felt. Cut wings from brown felt, body from light brown felt, small wing dots from gold felt, and large wing dots from red felt.

Use glue stick to tack dots and body to wings.

With black embroidery floss, whipstitch dots to wings, whipstitch wings to end of scarf, and body on top of wings.

Weave in all yarn ends.

THIS PROJECT WAS CREATED WITH

Paton's Classic Merino, 100% wool, 3.5oz/100g = 223yd/205m, 1 ball of color paprika (#238)

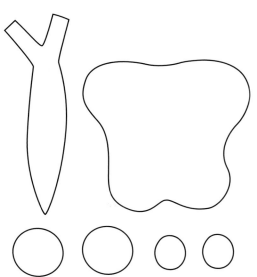

Enlarge 200%

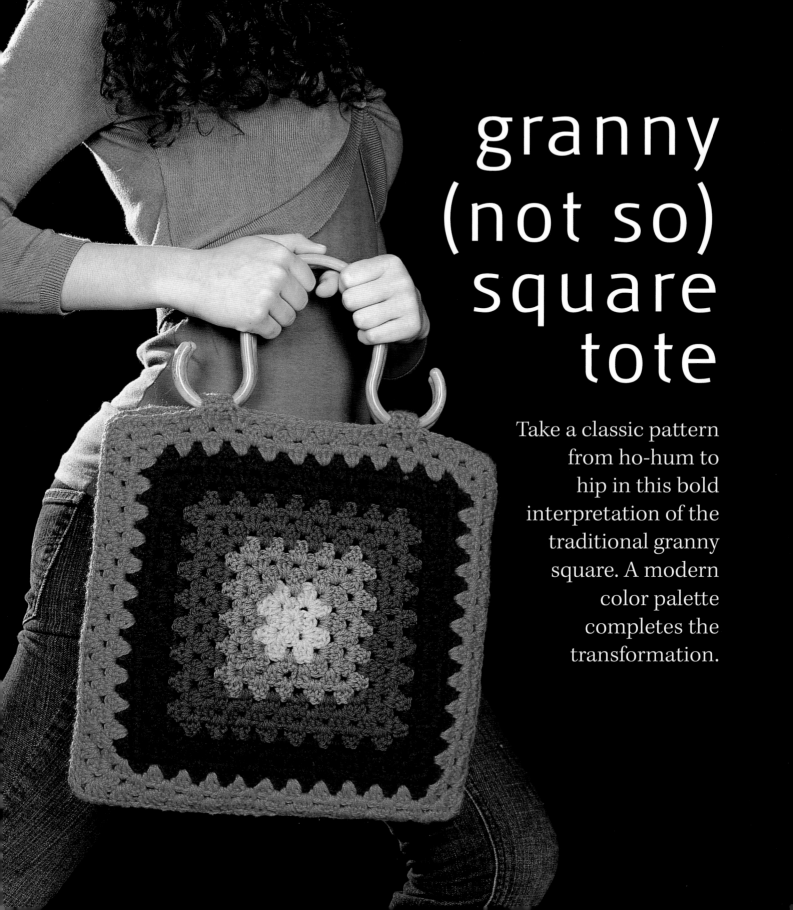

granny (not so) square tote

Take a classic pattern from ho-hum to hip in this bold interpretation of the traditional granny square. A modern color palette completes the transformation.

FINISHED MEASUREMENTS
14" square/36cm excluding handles

YOU WILL NEED
30yd/28m worsted weight yarn in gold (A)

55yd/50m worsted weight yarn in soft pink (B)

110yd/101m worsted weight yarn in blue/green (C)

140yd/128m worsted weight yarn in brown (D)

180yd/165m worsted weight yarn in bright pink (E)

Hook: 5.5mm/I-9 or size needed to obtain gauge

1yd/.9m felt in gray

1 pair curved wooden handles

Yarn needle

STITCHES USED
Chain (ch)

Double crochet (dc)

Half double crochet (hdc)

Slip stitch (sl st)

GAUGE
Take time to check your gauge.

First 4 rnds = 4"/10cm in diameter

PATTERN NOTE
To avoid unraveling, weave in yarn ends as work progresses.

GRANNY SQUARE (MAKE 2, 1 FOR EACH SIDE OF BAG)

With A, ch 4; join with sl st in first ch to form a ring.

Rnd 1 (right side): Ch 3 (counts as first dc here and throughout), 2 dc in ring, ch 1, *3 dc in ring, ch 1; repeat from * 2 more times; join with sl st in top of beginning ch-3 (4 ch-1 spaces).

Rnd 2 (wrong side): Ch 3, turn, (2 dc, ch 1, 3 dc) in first ch-1 space (corner made), ch 1, *(3 dc, ch 1, 3 dc) in next ch-1 space (corner made), ch 1; repeat from * 2 more times; join with sl st in top of beginning ch-3 (4 corners). Fasten off.

Join B with a sl st in any corner ch-1 space.

Rnd 3: Ch 3, turn, (2 dc, ch 1, 3 dc) in same corner ch-1 space, ch 1, *3 dc in next ch-1 space, ch 1, (3 dc, ch 1, 3 dc) in next corner ch-1 space, ch 1; repeat from * 2 more times, 3 dc in last ch-1 space, ch 1; join with sl st in top of beginning ch-3.

Rnd 4: Ch 3, turn, 2 dc in first ch-1 space, ch 1, 3 dc in next ch-1 space, ch 1, *(3 dc, ch 1, 3 dc) in next corner ch-1 space, (ch 1, 3 dc in next ch-1 space) across to next corner ch-1 space, ch 1; repeat from * 2 more times, (3 dc, ch 1, 3 dc) in last corner ch-1 space, ch 1; join with sl st in top of beginning ch-3.

Rnd 5: Ch 3, turn, 2 dc in first ch-1 space, ch 1, *(3 dc, ch 1, 3 dc) in next corner ch-1 space, (ch 1, 3 dc in next ch-1 space) across to next corner ch-1 space, ch 1; repeat from * 2 more times, (3 dc, ch 1, 3 dc) in next corner ch-1 space, (ch 1, 3 dc in next ch-1 space) across to beginning ch, ch 1; join with sl st in top of beginning ch-3. Fasten off.

Join C with a sl st in any corner ch-1 space.

Rnd 6: Ch 3, turn, (2 dc, ch 1, 3 dc) in same ch-1 space, (ch 1, 3 dc in next ch-1 space) across to next corner ch-1 space, ch 1, *(3 dc, ch 1, 3 dc) in next corner ch-1 space, (ch 1, 3 dc in next ch-1 space) across to next corner ch-1 space, ch 1; repeat from * 2 more times; join with sl st in top of beginning ch-3.

Rnd 7: Ch 3, turn, 2 dc in first ch-1 space, (ch 1, 3 dc in next ch-1 space) across to next corner ch-1 space, ch 1, *(3 dc, ch 1, 3 dc) in next corner ch-1 space, (ch 1, 3 dc in next ch-1 space) across to next corner ch-1 space, ch 1; repeat from * 2 more times, (3 dc, ch 1, 3 dc) in last corner ch-1 space, ch 1; join with sl st in top of beginning ch-3.

Rnds 8: Repeat Rnd 5.

Join D with a sl st in any corner ch-1 space.

Rnds 9–10: Repeat Rnds 6–7.

Rnd 11: Repeat Rnd 5.

Join E with a sl st in any corner ch-1 space.

Rnds 12–13: Repeat Rnds 6–7.

Rnd 14: Repeat Rnd 5.

HANDLE TAB (MAKE 4)

Note: Work two tabs on one edge (top) of each granny square.

Join E with sl st about 2"/5.1cm in from edge of granny square.

Row 1: Ch 2 (counts as first hdc here and throughout), hdc in next 4 sts (5 hdc).

Rows 2–5: Ch 2, turn, hdc in next 4 hdc.

Fasten off, leaving a 12"/31cm end for sewing.

Fold tab to the inside and sew last row to top of bag behind first row of tab. Repeat these instructions for 3 more tabs (2 on top edge of each granny square).

FINISHING

With E, whipstitch the lower edges (opposite edge with tabs) of the granny squares together.

LINE GRANNY SQUARE TOTE

Lay long rectangle of granny squares on top of felt on a flat surface. Trace around rectangle. Remove granny squares, measure 1"/2.5cm in from top edge and 1"/2.5cm in from right edge, and cut out rectangle of felt.

Lay felt rectangle centered on top of granny squares. There should be about ½"/1.3cm of granny square extending past all the edges of the felt rectangle.

Whipstitch edges of felt lining to granny squares. Make sure the stitches do not show on the front of the granny squares.

Fold crochet piece in half, bringing tabbed ends together. Whipstitch side seams together.

Weave in all yarn ends.

THIS PROJECT WAS CREATED WITH

Coats & Clark's Red Heart Classic, 100% acrylic, 3.5oz/99g = 190yd/174m

(A) 1 ball, color honey gold (#645)

(B) 1 ball, color cameo rose (#759)

(C) 1 ball, color teal (#48)

(D) 1 ball, color coffee (#365)

Coats & Clark's Red Heart Super Saver (Economy), 100% acrylic, 7oz/198g = 364yd/333m

(E) 1 ball, color shocking pink (#718)

ruffled roundabout striped scarf

FINISHED MEASUREMENTS
9" wide x 60" long/23cm x 153cm

YOU WILL NEED

160yd/146m of worsted weight yarn in purple (A)

160yd/146m of worsted weight yarn in soft pink (B)

160yd/146m of worsted weight yarn in bright pink (C)

240yd/220m of worsted weight yarn in brown (D)

Hook: 6mm/J-10 or size needed to obtain gauge

Yarn needle

STITCHES USED

Chain (ch)

Half double crochet (hdc)

Double crochet (dc)

Slip stitch (sl st)

GAUGE

Take time to check your gauge.

8 dc = 4"/10cm

7 rows = 4"/10cm

Feeling a downtown, heading-to-the-club vibe? Wear this striking piece; the luxe ruffle is formed by working multiple double crochet stitches in each space around the entire perimeter.

PATTERN NOTES

Double crochet stitches are worked in the spaces between stitches, not in the top of stitches. The last space is between the last stitch and the beginning chain of the previous row.

To change color, work last stitch to the last yarn over, yarn over with the new color, and draw through all loops on hook to complete the stitch. Fasten off old color.

SCARF

Ch 117.

Row 1: Hdc in 3rd ch from hook and in each ch across (115 hdc).

Row 2: Ch 3 (counts as first dc here and throughout), turn, *skip next space between sts, 2 dc in next space between sts; repeat from * across to last space, skip last space, dc in top of beginning ch-2.

Rows 3–4: Ch 3, turn, *skip next space between sts, 2 dc in next space between sts; repeat from * across to last space, skip last space, dc in top of beginning ch-3; change to B in last st of last row.

Rows 5–8: Repeat Row 3; change to C in last st of last row.

Rows 9–12: Repeat Row 3.

Fasten off.

RUFFLE

Join D with sl st in first ch on opposite side of foundation chain.

Rnd 1: Ch 3 (counts as first dc here and throughout), 3 dc in same st as join (corner made); 2 dc in each space between sts across, 4 dc in last ch (corner made); turn to work in ends of rows along short edge, 3 dc in end of each row across; turn to work across last row, 4 dc in first st (corner made), 2 dc in each space between sts across, 4 dc in last st (corner made) ; turn to work in ends of rows along short edge, 3 dc in end of each row across; join with sl st in top of beginning ch-3.

Rnd 2: Ch 3, *2 dc in next space between sts, dc in next space between sts; repeat from * around; join with sl st in top of beginning ch-3. Fasten off.

FINISHING

Weave in all yarn ends.

THIS PROJECT WAS CREATED WITH

Lion Brand's Wool-Ease Worsted Weight, 80% acrylic, 20% wool, 3oz/85g = 197yd/180m

(A) 1 ball, color grape heather (#144)

Coats & Clark's Red Heart Classic, 100% acrylic, 3.5oz/99g = 190yd/174m

(B) 1 ball, color medium coral (#252)

(C) 1 ball, color sea coral (#246)

Lion Brand's Wool-Ease Worsted Weight, 80% acrylic, 20% wool, 3oz/85g = 197yd/180m

(D) 1 ball, color chocolate brown (#126)

get lost

It's easy to see how this dynamite piece got its name; you could almost disappear in the vivid folds of this extra-long scarf. Crochet shells make for easy work and add an airy quality.

FINISHED MEASUREMENTS
10" wide x 95" long/25cm x 241cm excluding fringe

YOU WILL NEED
80yd/73m of worsted weight yarn in brown (A)

80yd/73m of worsted weight yarn in gold (B)

80yd/73m of worsted weight yarn in purple (C)

80yd/73m of worsted weight yarn in soft green (D)

80yd/73m of worsted weight yarn in blue (E)

80yd/73m of worsted weight yarn in soft yellow (F)

80yd/73m of worsted weight yarn in orange (G)

80yd/73m of worsted weight yarn in dark red (H)

80yd/73m of worsted weight yarn in bright green (I)

80yd/73m of worsted weight yarn in gray (J)

80yd/73m of worsted weight yarn in bright pink (K)

80yd/73m of worsted weight yarn blue/green (L)

80yd/73m of worsted weight yarn taupe (M)

Hook: 6mm/J-10 or size needed to obtain gauge

Yarn needle

13" wide/33cm piece of heavy cardboard

STITCHES USED
Chain (ch)

Half double crochet (hdc)

Double crochet (dc)

Single crochet (sc)

Shell: (2 dc, ch 1, 2 dc) in indicated stitch or space

GAUGE
Take time to check your gauge.

3 shells = 4"/10cm

5½ rows = 4"/10cm

PATTERN NOTE
To change color, work last stitch to the last yarn over, yarn over with the new color, and draw through all loops on hook to complete the stitch. Fasten off old color.

SCARF

With A, ch 45.

Row 1: Hdc in 3rd ch from hook and in each ch across (43 hdc)

Row 2: Ch 3 (counts as first dc here and throughout), turn, skip next 3 hdc, (2 dc, ch 1, 2 dc) in next hdc (shell made), *skip next 4 hdc, shell in next hdc; repeat from * across to last 3 sts, skip next 3 hdc, dc in top of beg ch-2 (8 shells).

Rows 3–13: Ch 3, turn; working in ch-1 spaces of shells, work 1 shell in each ch-1 space across; dc in top of beg ch-3; change to B in last st of last row.

Rows 14–25: Repeat Row 3; change to C in last st of last row.

Rows 26–37: Repeat Row 3; change to D in last st of last row.

Rows 38–49: Repeat Row 3; change to E in last st of last row.

Rows 50–61: Repeat Row 3; change to F in last st of last row.

Rows 62–73: Repeat Row 3; change to G in last st of last row.

Rows 74–85: Repeat Row 3; change to H in last st of last row.

Rows 86–97: Repeat Row 3; change to I in last st of last row.

Rows 98–109: Repeat Row 3; change to J in last st of last row.

Rows 110–121: Repeat Row 3; change to K in last st of last row.

Rows 122–133: Repeat Row 3.

Row 134: Ch 2 turn, hdc in each dc and ch-1 space across; hdc in top of beginning ch-3. Fasten off.

FINISHING

Weave in all yarn ends.

FRINGE

Wind L around 13"/33cm piece of heavy cardboard 6 times; wind M around 13"/33cm piece of heavy cardboard 30 times. Cut along 1 end of wraps to create 36 strands each about 26"/66cm long. Fold 1 strand of M in half. Using crochet hook, pull the folded end through the space between the first 2 stitches of the last row. Use the crochet hook to pull the cut ends through the fold. Repeat this process evenly, spacing 18 fringes across the row, interspersing the L fringe as desired. Then turn scarf and attach fringe in the same manner along the opposite end. Trim the ends of the fringe to even.

THIS PROJECT WAS CREATED WITH

Coats & Clark's Red Heart Soft, 100% acrylic, 5oz/140g = 256yd/234m

(A) 1 ball, color chocolate (#9344)

(C) 1 ball, color grape (#3729)

Coats & Clark's Red Heart Classic, 100% acrylic, 3.5oz/99g = 190yd/174m

(B) 1 ball, color honey gold (#645)

(D) 1 ball, color light sage (#631)

(E) 1 ball, color amethyst (#588)

(F) 1 ball, color maize (#261)

(G) 1 ball, color copper (#289)

(H) 1 ball, color cardinal (#917)

(J) 1 ball, color nickel (#401)

Coats & Clark's Red Heart Grandé, 100% acrylic, 6oz/170g = 143yd/130m

(I) 1 ball, color lime (#2652)

Coats & Clark's Red Heart Super Saver (Economy), 100% acrylic, 7oz/198g = 364yd/333m

(K) 1 ball, color shocking pink (#718)

Lion Brand's Wool-Ease Thick & Quick, 80% acrylic, 20% wool, 6oz/170g = 106yd/97m

(L) 1 ball, color teal (#170),

(M) 1 ball, color taupe (#122)

angled shell pompom hat

Bad hair day? Forget about it. Double crochets, angled shells, and pompoms conspire to offer you a most attractive solution.

SIZE
This hat is designed to fit most adult heads.

YOU WILL NEED
100yd/91m of worsted weight yarn in lavender (A)

35yd/32m of worsted weight yarn in medium green (B)

Hook: 10mm/N-15 or size needed to obtain gauge

Yarn needle

1½"/4cm pompom maker

STITCHES USED
Chain (ch)

Double crochet (dc)

Single crochet (sc)

Slip stitch (sl st)

Angled shell: (4 dc, ch 2, dc) in indicated space.

GAUGE
Take time to check your gauge.

First 3 rnds = 4"/10cm diameter

10 dc = 4"/10cm

2 angled shells = 4"/10cm

PATTERN NOTES
In Rnds 2–7, double crochet stitches are worked in the spaces between stitches, not in the top of stitches. The first space is between the beginning chain of the previous round and the next double crochet.

In Rnds 1–7, the work is not turned before starting each round.

In Rnds 8–11, the work is turned before starting each round.

HAT
With A, ch 3; join with sl st in first ch to form a ring.

Rnd 1: Ch 3 (counts as first dc here and throughout), work 8 more dc in ring; join with sl st in top of beginning ch-3 (9 dc).

Rnd 2: Ch 3, dc in first space between sts, *2 dc in next space between sts; repeat from * around; join with sl st in top of beginning ch-3 (18 dc).

Rnd 3: Ch 3, dc in first 2 spaces between sts, *2 dc in next space between sts, dc in next space between sts; repeat from * around; join with sl st in top of beginning ch-3 (27 dc).

Rnd 4: Ch 3, dc in first 3 spaces between sts, *2 dc in next space between sts, dc in next 2 spaces between sts; repeat from * around; join with sl st in top of beginning ch-3 (36 dc).

Rnd 5: Ch 3, dc in first 4 spaces between sts, *2 dc in next space between sts, dc in next 3 spaces between sts; repeat from * around; join with sl st in top of beginning ch-3 (45 dc).

Rnd 6: Ch 3, dc in each space around; join with sl st in top of beginning ch-3.

Rnd 7: Ch 6, skip first 4 spaces between sts, *(4 dc, ch 2, dc) in next space between sts (angled shell made), skip 3 spaces; repeat from * 3 more times; (4 dc, ch 2, dc) in next space between sts, skip 4 spaces; **(4 dc, ch 2, dc) in next space between sts, skip 3 spaces; repeat from ** 4 more times; join with sl st in 4th ch of beginning ch-6 (10 ch-2 spaces).

Note: Turn work to start Rnds 8–11. Work is completed in ch-2 spaces only, skip all stitches between the ch-2 spaces.

Rnds 8–11: Ch 3, turn, *(4 dc, ch 2, dc) in next ch-2 space; repeat from * around; join with sl st in top of beginning ch-3.

Fasten off.

Rnd 12: Join B with sl st in any st of Rnd 11, ch 1, sc in same st, sc in each dc and ch around; join with sl st in first sc. Fasten off.

FINISHING

POMPOM (MAKE 3)

With B, and your pompom maker, make 3 pompoms. With B, using photograph as a guide, sew pompoms in a cluster to lower side edge of hat.

Weave in all yarn ends.

THIS PROJECT WAS CREATED WITH

Coats & Clark's Red Heart Classic, 100% acrylic, 3.5oz/99g = 190yd/174m

(A) 1 ball, color lavender (#584

Brown Sheep Company's Lamb's Pride Worsted Weight, 85% wool, 15% mohair, 3.5oz/99g = 190yd/174m

(B) 1 skein, color limeade (#M120)

ruffled roundabout color-block scarf

Bright textured blocks of color and a flirty ruffle combine playfully in this vibrant scarf. The unique texture is created with a pattern of overlapping stitches.

FINISHED MEASUREMENTS

6" wide x 45" long/15cm x 114cm

YOU WILL NEED

100yd/91m of worsted weight yarn
in orange (A)

100yd/91m of worsted weight yarn
in blue (B)

100yd/91m of worsted weight yarn
in purple (C)

150yd/137m of worsted weight yarn
in deep red (D)

Hook: 5.5mm/I-9 or size needed to
obtain gauge

Yarn needle

STITCHES USED

Chain (ch)

Double crochet (dc)

Half double crochet (hdc)

Slip stitch (sl st)

Dc3tog (double crochet 3 sts together): [Yarn over, insert hook in next
st and draw up a loop, yarn over
and draw through 2 loops on
hook] 3 times, yarn over and draw
through all 4 loops on hook.

GAUGE

Take time to check your gauge.

7 dc3tog = 4"/10cm

5 rows = 4"/10cm

PATTERN NOTES

The stitch pattern is created by grouping 3 stitches together in an overlapping pattern. The first dc3tog of a row groups the first 3 stitches together. The next dc3tog
groups the last grouped stitch of the previous dc3tog with the next 2 stitches.

To change color, work last stitch to the last yarn over, yarn over with the new
color, and draw through all loops on hook to complete the stitch. Fasten off old
color.

SCARF

With A, ch 19.

Row 1: Hdc in 3rd ch from hook and in each ch across (17 hdc).

Row 2: Ch 4 (counts as first dc, ch 1 here and throughout), turn, dc3tog next 3 sts,
ch 1, *dc3tog previous st and next 2 sts, ch 1; repeat from * across, dc in last st (7
overlapping dc3tog).

Note: The first dc3tog in the following rows group the first (ch 1, dc3tog, ch1) series. The following dc3togs group the (previous ch 1, dc3tog, ch 1) series.

Rows 3–9: Ch 4, turn, dc3tog next 3 sts, ch 1, *dc3tog previous st and next 2 sts, ch 1; repeat from * across, dc in 3rd ch of beginning ch-4; change to B in last st of last row.

Fasten off.

Rows 10–18: Repeat Row 3; change to C in last st of last row.

Rows 19–27: Repeat Row 3; change to A in last st of last row.

Rows 28: Repeat Row 3.

Rows 29–54: Repeat Rows 2–27.

Fasten off.

RUFFLE

Join D with sl st in first ch on opposite side of foundation chain.

Rnd 1: Ch 3, 4 dc in same st as join (corner made); working along opposite side of foundation chain, 2 dc in each ch across to last ch, 5 dc in last ch (corner made); turn to work in ends of rows along long edge, 3 dc in end of each row across; turn to work across last row, 5 dc in first st (corner made), 2 dc in each st across to last st, 5 dc in last st (corner made); turn to work in ends of rows along long edge, 3 dc in end of each row across; join with sl st in top of beginning ch-3. Fasten off.

FINISHING

Weave in all yarn ends.

THIS PROJECT WAS CREATED WITH

Coats & Clark's Red Heart Soft Yarn, 100% acrylic, 5oz/140g = 256yd/234m

(A) 1 ball, color tangerine (#4422)

(B) 1 ball, color grape (#3729)

(D) 1 ball, color fuchsia (#9537)

Coats & Clark's Red Heart Grandé, 100% acrylic, 6oz/170g = 143yd/130m

(C) 1 ball, color country blue (#2883)

bobbled messenger bag

FINISHED MEASUREMENTS
9½" wide x 12½" high/24cm x 32cm excluding handle, after felting

YOU WILL NEED
575yd/526m of worsted weight felting wool in medium brown (A)

90yd/82m of worsted weight felting wool in medium green (B)

90yd/82m of worsted weight felting wool in fuchsia (C)

Hook: 6mm/J-10 or size needed to obtain gauge

Yarn needle

2 buttons, ½"-1"/13mm-25mm diameter (optional)

STITCHES USED
Chain (ch)

Half double crochet (hdc)

Bobble Stitch (Bbl): Yarn over, insert hook in indicated st, yarn over and draw up a loop, yarn over and draw through 2 loops on hook; [yarn over, insert hook in same st, yarn over and draw up a loop, yarn over and draw through 2 loops on hook] 4 times, yarn over and draw through all 6 loops on hook.

GAUGE
Take time to check your gauge.

16 dc = 4"/10cm before felting

11 rows = 4"/10cm before felting

Here's a bag that's certain to be noticed. The lively bobbles supply interest and texture, while felting makes this bag thick and sturdy.

PATTERN NOTES
To change color work last stitch to last yarn over (2 loops remaining on hook for double crochet, 6 loops on hook for Bobble stitch), yarn over with new color and draw through all loops on hook to complete the stitch. Drop, but do not cut, old color. Carry old color beneath stitches of new color to next color change or end of row.

The results of felting can vary greatly and are dependent upon the type and color of wool used, water temperature and quality, the washing machine used, and the amount of time and agitation to which the piece is subjected.

BAG
With A, ch 49.

Row 1: Hdc in 3rd ch from hook and in each ch across (47 hdc).

Rows 2–3: Ch 2, turn, hdc in each hdc across.

Row 4: Ch 2, turn, hdc in first 5 hdc, *change to B, Bbl in next st, change to A, hdc in next 5 hdc; repeat from * across.

Rows 5–7: Repeat Row 2.

Row 8: Ch 2, turn, hdc in first 5 hdc, *change to C, Bbl in next st, change to A, hdc in next 5 hdc; repeat from * across.

Row 9–11: Repeat Row 2.

Row 12: Repeat Row 4.

Rows 13–36: Repeat Rows 5–12.

Rows 37–48: Repeat Row 2.

Rows 49: Repeat Row 4.

Rows 50–81: Repeat Rows 5–12.

Rows 82–84: Repeat Row 2.

Fasten off.

SHOULDER STRAP
With A, ch 8.

Row 1: Hdc in 3rd ch from hook and in each ch across (6 hdc).

Rows 2–110: Ch 2, turn, hdc in each hdc across.

Fasten off.

FELTING

You can felt the body of the bag and shoulder strap in the same wash cycle but you must place them in separate bags. This prevents the two pieces from felting together. Placing items for felting in bags also protects your washing machine from excessive lint.

Felting time varies according to the washing machine, water condition, and the color of the wool.

Weave in all yarn ends before felting. Place body of bag and shoulder strap in two separate zippered lingerie bags or pillow protectors. Set your washer to hot water, a low water level, and the highest agitation setting. Place pieces to be felted, along with an old pair of jeans for additional agitation, into the washer and add laundry detergent for a normal-sized load.

Run wash cycle, stopping cycle occasionally to check progress. It may take several wash cycles to achieve the desired result. When the desired level of density and degree of shrinkage is achieved, remove pieces from washer and rinse until the water runs clear.

Carefully shape the felted pieces and lay flat on a sweater rack to dry. Drying time varies. It may take a couple of days!

FINISHING

If felted pieces appear uneven, block lightly before assembling.

Fold the body of the bag in half, bringing first row up to meet last row. With A, whipstitch side edges together.

Line up top of one side seam of bag with center of one end of shoulder strap. With A, securely sew the end of the strap to the body of the bag. Taking care not to twist strap, repeat with the other end of the strap.

(Optional) Sew one button over each end of strap.

Weave in all yarn ends.

THIS PROJECT WAS CREATED WITH

Paton's Classic Merino, 100% wool, 3.5oz/100g = 223yd/205m

(A) 3 balls, color chestnut brown (#231)

Brown Sheep Company's Lamb's Pride Worsted Weight, 85% wool, 15% mohair, 3.5oz/99g = 190yd/174m

(B) 1 skein, color fuchsia (#M23)

(C) 1 skein, color turkish olive (#M41)

ribbons in the sky

Add sparkle to a plain raspberry beret with some shiny embellishment. It's a perfect project to use up those scraps of leftover ribbon yarn.

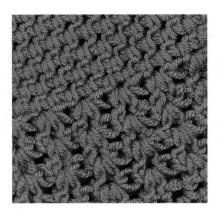

SIZE

This hat is designed to fit most adult heads.

YOU WILL NEED

110yd/101m of worsted weight yarn in medium pink (A)

40yd/37m of worsted weight ribbon yarn in blue/red/purple multicolor (B)

Hook: 3.25mm/D-3 or size needed to obtain gauge

Yarn needle

STITCHES USED

Chain (ch)

Half double crochet (hdc)

Single crochet (sc)

Slip stitch (sl st)

GAUGE

Take time to check your gauge.

First 7 rnds = 4"/10cm diameter

14 hdc = 4"/10cm

PATTERN NOTES

Half double crochet stitches are worked in the spaces between stitches, not in the tops of stitches. The first space is between the beginning chain of the previous round and the next half double crochet.

HAT

With A, ch 3; join with sl st in first ch to form a ring.

Rnd 1: Ch 2 (counts as first hdc here and throughout), work 6 more hdc in ring; join with sl st in top of beginning ch-2 (7 hdc).

Rnd 2: Ch 2, hdc in first space between sts, *2 hdc in next space between sts; repeat from * around; join with sl st in top of beginning ch-2 (14 hdc).

Rnd 3: Ch 2, hdc in first 2 spaces between sts, 2 hdc in next space between sts, *hdc in next space between sts, 2 hdc in next space between sts; repeat from * around to last space between sts, skip last space between sts; join with sl st in top of beginning ch-2 (20 hdc).

Rnd 4: Ch 2, hdc in first 3 spaces between sts, 2 hdc in next space between sts, *hdc in next 2 spaces between sts, 2 hdc in next space between sts; repeat from * around to last space between sts, skip last space between sts; join with sl st in top of beginning ch-2 (26 hdc).

Rnd 5: Ch 2, hdc in first 4 spaces between sts, 2 hdc in next space between sts, *hdc in next 3 spaces between sts, 2 hdc in next space between sts; repeat from * around to last space between sts, skip last space between sts; join with sl st in top of beginning ch-2 (32 hdc).

Rnd 6: Ch 2, hdc in first 5 spaces between sts, 2 hdc in next space between sts, *hdc in next 4 spaces between sts, 2 hdc in next space between sts; repeat from * around to last space between sts, skip last space between sts; join with sl st in top of beginning ch-2 (38 hdc).

Rnd 7: Ch 2, hdc in first 6 spaces between sts, 2 hdc in next space between sts, *hdc in next 5 spaces between sts, 2 hdc in next space between sts; repeat from * around to last space between sts, skip last space between sts; join with sl st in top of beginning ch-2 (44 hdc).

Rnd 8: Ch 2, hdc in first 7 spaces between sts, 2 hdc in next space between sts, *hdc in next 6 spaces between sts, 2 hdc in next space between sts; repeat from * around to last space between sts, skip last space between sts; join with sl st in top of beginning ch-2 (50 hdc).

Rnd 9: Ch 2, hdc in first 8 spaces between sts, 2 hdc in next space between sts, *hdc in next 7 spaces between sts, 2 hdc in next space between sts; repeat from * around to last space between sts, skip last space between sts; join with sl st in top of beginning ch-2 (56 hdc).

Rnd 10: Ch 2, hdc in first 9 spaces between sts, 2 hdc in next space between sts, *hdc in next 8 spaces between sts, 2 hdc in next space between sts; repeat from * around to last space between sts, skip last space between sts; join with sl st in top of beginning ch-2 (62 hdc).

Rnd 11: Ch 2, hdc in first 10 spaces between sts, 2 hdc in next space between sts, *hdc in next 9 spaces between sts, 2 hdc in next space between sts; repeat from * around to last space between sts, skip last space between sts; join with sl st in top of beginning ch-2 (68 hdc).

Rnds 12–16: Ch 2, hdc in each space between sts around; join with sl st in top of beginning ch-2 (68 hdc).

Rnds 17–20: Ch 3 (counts as first dc here and throughout), dc in first space between sts, *skip next space between sts, 2 dc in next space between sts; repeat from * around to last space between sts, skip last space between sts; join with sl st in top of beginning ch-3.

Rnd 21: Ch 2, hdc in each st around; join with sl st in top of beginning ch-2. Fasten off.

Join B with sl st in same st as join.

Rnd 22–24: Ch 2, hdc in each st around; join with sl st in top of beginning ch-2. Fasten off.

FLOWER

With A, ch 3; join with sl st in first ch to form a ring.

Rnd 1: Ch 3 (counts as first dc here and throughout), work 9 more dc in ring; join with sl st in top of beginning ch-3 (10 dc). Fasten off.

Join B with sl st in any dc of Rnd 1.

Rnd 2: Ch 6 (counts as dc, ch 3), *skip next dc, dc in next dc, ch 3; repeat from * around; join with sl st in 3rd ch of beginning ch-6 (5 ch-3 spaces).

Rnd 3: (Sl st, hdc, 3 dc, hdc, sl st) in each ch-3 space around (5 petals).

Rnd 4: Working in front of Rnd 3 petals, ch 2, skip next dc of Rnd 1, *sl st around post of next dc of Rnd 1, ch 2, skip next dc of Rnd 1; repeat from * around; join with sl st in first ch of beginning ch-2 (5 ch-2 spaces).

Rnd 5: (Sl st, hdc, 2 dc, hdc, sl st) in each ch-2 space around (5 petals). Fasten off.

FINISHING

Sew flower to side of lower edge of hat. Weave in all yarn ends.

THIS PROJECT WAS CREATED WITH

Debbie Bliss' Cathay, 50% cotton, 35% viscose microfiber, 15% silk, 1.76oz/50g = 109yd/100m

(A) 1 ball, color #10

Moda Dea's Spellbound, 83% nylon, 17% polyester, 1.76oz/50g = 85yd/93m

(B) 1 ball, color majesty (#2724)

mohair delight

This scarf is quietly chic, worked in calming shades of ultra-soft mohair yarn that give a sophisticated makeover to this traditional stitch pattern.

FINISHED MEASUREMENTS
4" wide x 48" long/10cm x 122cm

YOU WILL NEED
100yd/91m sport weight yarn in
    lavender (A)

150yd/136m sport weight yarn in
    dark green (B)

Hook: 5.5mm/I-9 or size needed to
    obtain gauge

Yarn needle

STITCHES USED
Chain (ch)

Double crochet (dc)

Slip stitch (sl st)

GAUGE
Take time to check your gauge.

1 granny square = 4"/10cm in diam-
    eter.

PATTERN NOTE
To avoid unraveling, weave in yarn ends as work progresses.

GRANNY SQUARE (MAKE 12)

With A, ch 4; join with sl st in first ch to form a ring.

Rnd 1 (right side): Ch 3 (counts as first dc here and throughout), 2 dc in ring, ch 1, *3 dc in ring, ch 1; repeat from * 2 more times; join with sl st in top of beginning ch-3 (4 ch-1 spaces).

Rnd 2 (wrong side): Ch 3, turn, (2 dc, ch 1, 3 dc) in first ch-1 space (corner made), ch 1, *(3 dc, ch 1, 3 dc) in next ch-1 space (corner made), ch 1; repeat from * 2 more times; join with sl st in top of beginning ch-3 (4 corners). Fasten off.

Join B with a sl st in any corner ch-1 space.

Rnd 3: Ch 3, turn, (2 dc, ch 1, 3 dc) in same corner ch-1 space, ch 1, *3 dc in next ch-1 space, ch 1, (3 dc, ch 1, 3 dc) in next corner ch-1 space, ch 1; repeat from * 2 more times, 3 dc in last ch-1 sp, ch 1; join with sl st in top of beginning ch-3.

Rnd 4: Ch 3, turn, 2 dc in first ch-1 space, ch 1, 3 dc in next ch-1 space, ch 1, *(3 dc, ch 1, 3 dc) in next corner ch-1 space, (ch 1, 3 dc in next ch-1 space) across to next corner ch-1 space, ch 1; repeat from * 2 more times, (3 dc, ch 1, 3 dc) in last corner ch-1 space, ch 1; join with sl st in top of beginning ch-3. Fasten off leaving a 12"/30.5cm end for sewing.

FINISHING

Using yarn ends, whipstitch granny squares together along edges to make a long strip.

Weave in all yarn ends.

THIS PROJECT WAS CREATED WITH

GGH's Soft-Kid, 70% super kid mohair, 25% nylon, 5% wool, 0.88oz/25g = 151yd/138m

(A) 1 ball, color #13

GGH's Soft-Kid in color #54, 70% super kid mohair, 25% nylon, 5% wool, 0.88oz/25g = 151yd/138m

(B) 1 ball, color #54

wineberry kiss

FINISHED MEASUREMENTS
6" long x 21" upper circumference x 41" lower circumference/15cm x 53cm x 104cm

YOU WILL NEED
75yd/69m of bulky weight yarn in deep purple (A)

20yd/18m of bulky weight textured yarn in fuchsia (B)

Hook: 6.5mm/K-10.5 or size needed to obtain gauge

Yarn needle

STITCHES USED
Chain (ch)

Double crochet (dc)

Single crochet (sc)

Slip stitch (sl st)

V-stitch (V-st): (dc, ch 1, dc) in indicated ch-space.

GAUGE
Take time to check your gauge.

6 (dc, ch 1) repeats = 4"/10cm

6 rows = 4"/10cm

Create some buzz with this cool collar, dressing it up or down. Wineberry Kiss is worked in rounds of double crochet, and simple V-stitches provide the increases while adding to the lacy look.

COLLAR

With A, ch 54; taking care to not twist the chain, join with sl st in first ch to form a ring.

Rnd 1: Ch 4 (counts as first dc, ch 1), (skip next ch, dc in next ch, ch 1) 2 times, skip next ch, *(dc, ch 1, dc) in next ch (V-st made), ch 1, skip next ch, (dc in next ch, ch 1, skip next ch) 5 times; repeat from * around; join with sl st in 3rd ch of beginning ch-4 (31 ch-1 space).

Rnd 2: Ch 4 (counts as first dc, ch 1), dc in first ch-1 space (beginning V-st made), ch 1, (dc in next ch-1 space, ch 1) 4 times, *V-st in next ch-1 space, ch 1, (dc in next ch-1 space, ch 1) 4 times; repeat from * around to last ch-1 space, dc in last ch-1 space, ch 1; join with sl st in 3rd ch of beginning ch-4 (37 ch-1 space).

Rnd 3: Ch 4 (counts as first dc, ch 1), dc in first ch-1 space (beginning V-st made), ch 1, (dc in next ch-1 space, ch 1) across to next V-st, *V-st in ch-1 space of V-st, ch 1, (dc in next ch-1 space, ch 1) across to next V-st; repeat from * around; join with sl st in 3rd ch of beginning ch-4 (43 ch-1 space).

Rnds 4–6: Repeat Rnd 3 (61 ch-1 space).

Rnd 7: Ch 4 (counts as first dc, ch 1), *dc in next ch-1 space, ch 1; repeat from * around; join with sl st in 3rd ch of beginning ch-4. Fasten off.

Join B with sc in any ch-1 space.

Rnd 8: Ch 8, *sc in next ch-1 space, ch 8; repeat from * around; join with sl st in first sc. Fasten off.

FINISHING

Weave in all yarn ends.

THIS PROJECT WAS CREATED WITH

Karabella's Aurora Bulky, 100% extra fine merino, 1.75oz/50g = 54yd/49m

(A) 2 balls, color #26

Lion Brand's Homespun, 98% acrylic, 2% polyester, 6oz/170g = 185yd/169m

(B) 1 ball, color fuchsia #385

let's get technical

FIGURE 1

Before we get hooking, it is important to make sure we are on the same page, especially when it comes to sharing a common technical reference point. On the following pages, you'll find a review of the stitches and techniques used to create the projects in *Crochet Chic*. If you are a novice stitcher you may want to spend some extra time browsing this section. If you're a seasoned loopanista, you may choose to refer to it, if need be, while you work your projects. Let's review (or preview, as the case may be).

FIGURE 2

GET A GRIP—HOLDING THE HOOK

There are probably more ways to hold a crochet hook than there are ways to skin a cat. While finding a comfortable hook-holding position comes through experimentation, the two most commonly used holds are the pencil hold (figure 1), and the knife hold (figure 2). The main objective of both holds is to maintain a comfortable grasp of the hook.

FIGURE 3

THE SLIPKNOT—ATTACHING YOUR YARN

In order to get your yarn onto the hook, you will need to create a slipknot. This is easily done by following these simple steps.

MAKING A SLIPKNOT

1. Make a loop of yarn with a 6"/15cm tail.

2. With the yarn connected to the skein hanging behind the loop, use the head of the hook to catch the yarn that is coming from your skein and pull it through the loop (figure 3).

Secure your slipknot by pulling gently on both ends of the yarn (figure 4).

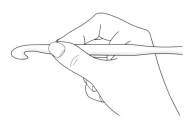

FIGURE 4

GET A GRIP—HOLDING YOUR YARN

Learning how to hold your yarn sounds really easy, but learning how to hold it properly can prove to be quite tricky. As with most crochet techniques, there are many ways to hold yarn effectively, but a basic and simple yarn hold can be achieved by doing the following:

HOLDING THE YARN

1. Holding the yarn in the hand in which you are not holding the hook, clutch the yarn with a bent pinky finger.

2. Drape the yarn that is running under your palm over your index finger (figure 5).

FIGURE 5

3. Grip the tail of the yarn that's on the hook between your thumb and middle finger (figure 6).

Now you're poised to get hooking!

FIGURE 6

A MATTER OF ATTITUDE

If there's one thing I learned while working with entertainers, it's the value of attitude. Wear your creation proudly, and with a little sass, if you want. Even the simplest of accessories can add flair and drama to your daywear. A simple tee and pair of jeans become a fashion statement with the addition of a sophisticated scarf.

An elegant but easily made wrap, shawl, or cowl can light up your eveningwear. A runway strut completes the ensemble!

basic
crochet stitches

Crochet projects are worked in either a series of rows or a series of rounds, beginning with a chain stitch *foundation chain*. Many different stitches are used to create these rounds and rows. You need to know only five basic crochet stitches to complete the projects in this book: chain stitch, slip stitch, single crochet, half double crochet, and double crochet. Using these basic stitches, you will be amazed at the variety of looks you can achieve.

One of the most important differences between the different crochet stitches is the relative height of each stitch. Slip stitches are very short, single crochet stitches are a bit taller, and double crochet stitches are about twice as tall as single crochet stitches. A half double crochet stitch is taller than a single crochet but shorter than a double crochet. In general, the taller the stitch you use: 1) the faster your project will be finished, 2) the more "lacey" your project will be, and 3) the more loose and drapey your project will be. In addition, the height of the stitch being used determines how many chains you will need to work before starting the next row of stitches.

A LITTLE WORD—ABBREVIATIONS

Crochet instructions use abbreviations for stitch names and crochet steps. As stitches are introduced, the abbreviation for each stitch and step will be given in parentheses following the name of the stitch or step. The number of abbreviations used in this book has been kept to a minimum. When you encounter an abbreviation you don't know, refer to the handy chart at the right (figure 7).

ABBREVIATIONS

CH	CHAIN
DC	DOUBLE CROCHET
DC3TOG	DOUBLE CROCHET 3 STITCHES TOGETHER
HDC	HALF DOUBLE CROCHET
RND	ROUND
SC	SINGLE CROCHET
SC2TOG	SINGLE CROCHET 2 STITCHES TOGETHER
SL ST	SLIP STITCH
ST (S)	STITCH(ES)

FIGURE 7

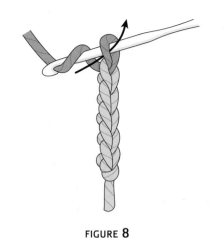

FIGURE **8**

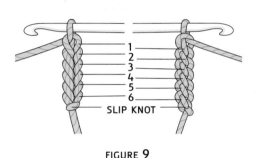

FIGURE **9**

MAKING YOUR CHAIN

The chain stitch (ch) is the most basic stitch in the art of crochet. A series of chain stitches makes up the foundation chain of every project you will crochet. Begin your chain by following these simple steps.

CHAIN STITCH (CH)

1. Make a slipknot.

2. Carry the yarn over the hook from the back to the front.

3. Catch the yarn with the hook, and draw it through the loop on the hook.

You have now made one chain stitch. Repeat Steps 2 and 3 to create additional chain stitches (figure 8).

THE ONLY STITCH IS THE STITCH THAT COUNTS— COUNTING YOUR CHAIN STITCHES

As I said before, a crochet project begins with a foundation chain that is made up of a series of chain stitches. Each pattern that you will work calls for a specific number of chain stitches. It can be difficult, and sometimes confusing, to determine exactly how many chain stitches you have made. In order to take an accurate count of your chain stitches you will first need to know which side of the chain is the front and which side is the back.

The front side has the appearance of a series of vertically stacked "V's".

The back side has the appearance of a vertically stacked ridge of loops, known as back bumps or back bars.

In order to count your stitches, turn the front side of the chain towards you, and excluding the loop on the hook (as well as the slipknot), count only the series of "V's" (figure 9).

Notice that the loop on the hook never counts as a stitch. I advise you to begin counting with the first chain after the loop on the hook. Project instructions often tell you to work a stitch in the second, third, or fourth chain from the hook. To determine which chain to work into, begin counting with the first chain after the loop on the hook and count up as you move away from the hook.

A MATTER OF DESIGN

While many of my projects are rather simple to make, the use of color, proportion, and embellishment take them from ordinary to extraordinary.

I guess you could say I'm hooked on color (pun fully intended). Although there are many important considerations when designing and working a crocheted piece, color is the most important consideration of all, in my opinion. I feel that the significance of color supersedes technical ability, since it's completely possible to design and work a beautiful piece using a very basic stitch—it's the stylish color combinations that make it extra special. Although texture is also important, you can make a visual compensation for texture by mimicking it with a careful yarn choice. You can also eliminate the need for texture altogether by using the right color combination.

The combinations of colors for the projects worked in this book are built around my own personal philosophy of grounding, anchoring, or muting brighter or lighter color groupings, and conversely adding lift and vibrancy to darker color groupings. This interplay of color helps create a mood of overall sophisticated balance and elegance.

SLIP STITCH

The slip stitch (sl st) is the shortest stitch. Because the slip stitch is short it takes a long time to make an entire piece out of slip stitches. You won't find many patterns that use slip stitches extensively. Instead, the slip stitch is most useful when changing colors and joining rounds.

FIGURE 10

SLIP STITCH (SL ST)

1. Work a foundation chain of any length.

2. Insert the hook in the second chain from the hook (figure 10).

FIGURE 11

3. Carry the yarn over the hook and pull the yarn through the chain stitch and through the loop on the hook (figure 11).

You have now made a slip stitch. Insert the hook in the next stitch and repeat Step 3 to create additional slip stitches.

FIGURE 12

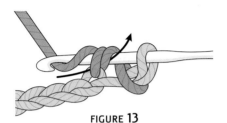

FIGURE 13

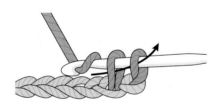

FIGURE 14

FIGURE 15

REACHING THE END OF A ROW—TURN, TURN, TURN

So you've completed a row of crochet stitches, now what? You need to turn your work and stitch across the row you just completed. Turning your work in crochet is easy: you simply turn the work and work the correct number of chain stitches, the turning chain. But first you have a decision to make—which stitch will you work in this next row? The height of the next stitch determines the number of chain stitches you must work before starting the next row. If the next stitch is a slip stitch or single crochet, you need to make one chain stitch before starting the next row. If the next stitch is a half double crochet, you need to make two chain stitches before starting the next row. And, if the next stitch is a double crochet, you need to make three chain stitches before starting the next row.

The turning chain is sometimes used as the first stitch in a row or round. The project instructions will tell you if the turning chain is counted as the first stitch. When the turning chain is used as the first stitch in a row or round, the first stitch in the previous row is skipped before working the next stitch, and the last stitch of the row is worked in the top of the turning chain of the previous row.

SINGLE CROCHET

Single crochet (sc) is the most commonly used stitch and is slightly taller than the slip stitch. While it is often used on its own, it can also be combined with other stitches to create pattern stitches, to create a variety of textures and laces.

SINGLE CROCHET (SC)

1. Work a foundation chain of any length.

2. Insert the hook in the second chain from the hook (figure 12).

3. Carry the yarn over the hook, from the back to the front, and pull the yarn back through the chain stitch (figure 13). You now have two loops on the crochet hook.

4. Carry the yarn over the hook one more time and pull it through both loops on the hook (figure 14).

You should have one loop remaining on the hook. You have now made one single crochet stitch (figure 15).

Insert the hook in the next stitch and repeat Steps 3 and 4 to create additional single crochet stitches.

HALF DOUBLE CROCHET

Half double crochet (hdc) might be considered the halfway stitch between single crochet and double crochet. It is widely used and easily worked.

HALF DOUBLE CROCHET (HDC)

1. Work a foundation chain of any length.

2. Carry your yarn over the hook, and insert the hook into the third chain from the hook (figure 16)

3. Carry your yarn over the crochet hook again and pull the yarn back through the chain stitch. You now have three loops on the crochet hook (figure 17).

4. Carry the yarn over the hook again and pull it through all three loops on the hook (figure 18). You should have one loop remaining on the hook.

You have now made a half double crochet stitch (figure 19).

Carry the yarn over the hook, insert the hook in the next stitch and repeat Steps 3 and 4 to create additional half double crochet stitches.

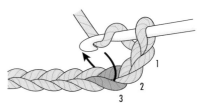

FIGURE 16

FIGURE 17

FIGURE 18

FIGURE 19

DOUBLE CROCHET

Double crochet (dc) is a taller stitch than the previous stitches discussed. Using it allows your crochet project to grow more quickly.

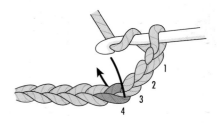

FIGURE 20

DOUBLE CROCHET (DC)

1. Work a foundation chain of any length.

2. Carry your yarn over the hook, and insert the hook into the fourth chain from the hook (figure 20)

3. Carry your yarn over the crochet hook and pull it back through the chain stitch. You now have three loops on the crochet hook (figure 21).

4. Carry the yarn over the hook and pull it through the first two loops on the crochet hook (figure 22). You now have two loops on the hook.

5. Carry the yarn over the hook one last time and pull it through the remaining two loops on the hook (figure 23). You should have one loop remaining on the hook.

You have now made a double crochet stitch (figure 24).

Carry the yarn over the hook, insert the hook in the next stitch, and repeat Steps 3 through 5 to create additional double crochet stitches.

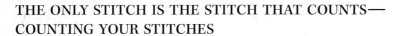

FIGURE 21

FIGURE 22

THE ONLY STITCH IS THE STITCH THAT COUNTS— COUNTING YOUR STITCHES

Slip, single crochet, half double crochet, and double crochet stitches can be counted in a manner similar to counting chain stitches (page 110). Angle your work so that you can look down on the top of the last row or round worked. You should see a series of V's that looks like the front of a series of chains. A count of the V's tells you the number of crochet stitches you worked in the last row or round. It is a good idea to count your stitches from time to time. The project instructions indicate the number of stitches you should have at different times throughout construction.

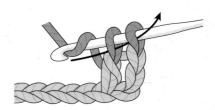

FIGURE 23

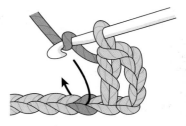

FIGURE 24

basic crochet techniques

In addition to knowing how to create a variety of crochet stitches, you will also need to learn some basic techniques to complete the projects in Crochet Chic. Basic crochet techniques allow you to join a new skein of yarn when the current skein runs out, change colors, shape your pieces using increases and decreases, work in rounds, fasten off when you finish your piece, and finish off neatly.

JOINING A NEW SKEIN OF YARN

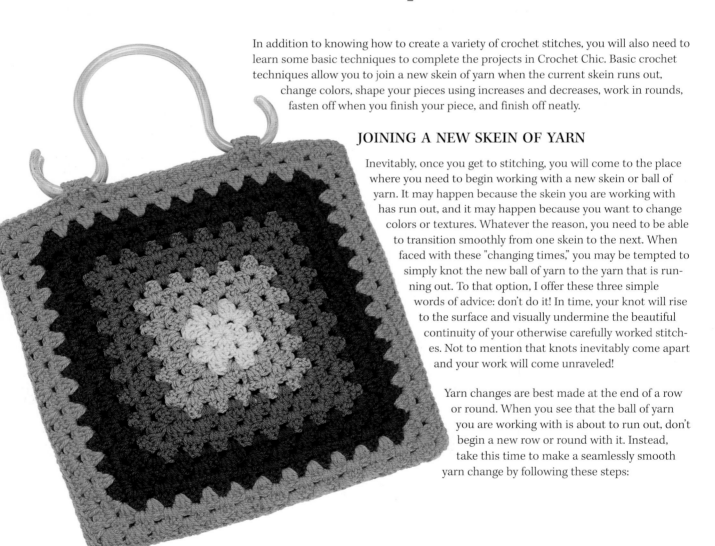

Inevitably, once you get to stitching, you will come to the place where you need to begin working with a new skein or ball of yarn. It may happen because the skein you are working with has run out, and it may happen because you want to change colors or textures. Whatever the reason, you need to be able to transition smoothly from one skein to the next. When faced with these "changing times," you may be tempted to simply knot the new ball of yarn to the yarn that is running out. To that option, I offer these three simple words of advice: don't do it! In time, your knot will rise to the surface and visually undermine the beautiful continuity of your otherwise carefully worked stitches. Not to mention that knots inevitably come apart and your work will come unraveled!

Yarn changes are best made at the end of a row or round. When you see that the ball of yarn you are working with is about to run out, don't begin a new row or round with it. Instead, take this time to make a seamlessly smooth yarn change by following these steps:

JOINING A NEW SKEIN OF YARN

1. Work the last stitch on your row or round to the last yarn over.

2. Use the hook to catch the new yarn and pull it through the remaining loops on the hook (figure 25).

3. Gently pull on the tails of the new and old yarn to make sure that the new loop is secure, and begin working your next row or round, using the new ball of yarn.

Note: Be sure to leave a 5-6"/13-15cm tail on both the new and old yarn, then weave the tails in when you get to the finishing stage.

To change yarn for a color change, you can't always wait until you reach the end of a row or round. Instead, work the above steps and leave the yarn tails on the back side of the work. Weave the tails in when you get to the finishing stage. If you are working a row or round that changes colors frequently, you can hide the yarn not in use by working the next few stitches over and around the yarn not in use. This technique is called carrying the yarn and it reduces the number of yarn tails you will need to weave in during the finishing stage. But, be careful not to pull the carried yarn too tight because this may cause your work to pucker.

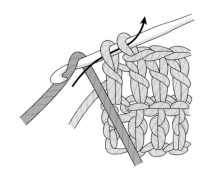

FIGURE 25

INCREASING AND DECREASING

Increasing and decreasing techniques are used to shape a garment or piece. Increases and decreases can take place anywhere within a row or round. Increases are achieved by simply working a designated number of stitches into the same stitch, thus increasing the total number of stitches (figure 26).

A typical crochet instruction for an increase is 2 sc in next st. This instruction indicates that two single crochets should be worked in the next stitch, rather than just one.

Decreases are worked just as simply, by working one stitch spanning over several stitches, thus decreasing the total number of stitches (figure 27). A decrease can be worked in any stitch (e.g. sc, hdc, and dc).

FIGURE 26

DECREASING

1. Insert hook into first stitch to be spanned, work a stitch to the last yarn over (but do not work the yarn over), leaving an extra loop on the hook.

2. Insert hook into the next stitch to be spanned, work another stitch to the last yarn over (but do not work the yarn over), again leaving an extra loop on the hook.

3. Repeat Step 2 to span as many stitches as desired.

4. Yarn over and draw through all loops on the hook, thus combining all the stitches into one stitch.

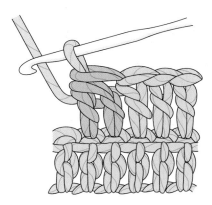

FIGURE 27

A typical crochet instruction for a decrease is sc2tog. This instruction indicates that a single crochet should be worked spanning the next two stitches (decreasing by one stitch). Similarly, dc3tog indicates that a double crochet should be worked spanning the next three stitches (decreasing by two stitches). The tog in sc2tog and dc3tog stands for together.

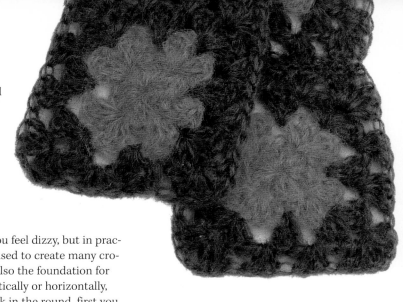

WORKING IN THE ROUND

The term "working in the round" may be enough to make you feel dizzy, but in practice, working in the round is quite easy and that's why it is used to create many crocheted items, most often hats, bags, toys, and flowers. It is also the foundation for making granny squares. Unlike projects that are worked vertically or horizontally, these projects are worked in rounds instead of rows. To work in the round, first you form the foundation chain into a ring, then you work a number of stitches into the ring to form the first round. Subsequent rounds are worked into the stitches of the first round. The number of stitches increased in each round determines the shape of the piece, which may be flat as in the medallion of Medallion Clutch, slightly rounded as in Flapper Girl, or rippled as in Hair Blossom.

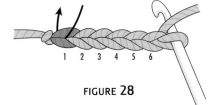

FIGURE **28**

WORKING IN THE ROUND

1. Begin by crocheting 6 chain stitches. The exact number of chains needed for each project is given in the instructions for each project (figure 28).

2. Join the last stitch you worked to the first stitch of the chain by inserting the hook in the first stitch and working a slip stitch. You have just formed a ring (figure 29).

3. Chain 1, insert the hook into the middle of the ring, and work the designated number of stitches (figure 30).

4. Join the last stitch of the round to the first stitch by working a slip stitch. You have now begun working in the round.

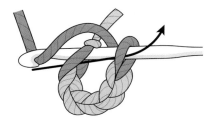

FIGURE **29**

LAST STOP ON THE CROCHET ASSEMBLY LINE— FINISHING IT ALL OFF

I just love the thrill of starting a new crochet project (to tell the truth, I've started a few more than I've finished), but the real thrill comes in seeing the project come together in a wondrous culmination. Once you've worked the last crochet stitch of your project, you'll need to polish things up with a few finishing and assembling touches.

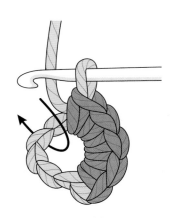

FIGURE **30**

FASTENING OFF

You're at the end of the last row or round of your project, now what? Fasten off. To fasten off, simply cut the yarn, leaving at least a 6"/15cm long tail for weaving in or sewing, and draw the end all the way through the last loop on the hook (figure 31). Gently tighten this final knot. That's it! What could be simpler?

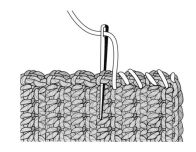

FIGURE **31**

THE GOOD OLD WHIPSTITCH

Many of these projects call for a bit of needle and thread assembly. The most effective stitch for these projects is the whipstitch. Line up the project piece(s) according to the specific instructions. Use your yarn needle, along with the yarn from the project, to carefully sew the pieces together from back to front. Insert needle from back to front through one loop of each piece and draw the yarn through, leaving at least a 6"/15.2cm yarn tail. Continue working whipstitches by bringing yarn and needle over the work to insert needle again from back to front for the next stitch (figure 32).

FIGURE **32**

SNIP AND TUCK

The final step in the assembly of the projects calls for a little tuck here and a little snip there. Thread the yarn tails onto your yarn needle then carefully weave them into the body of your stitching until only a very short tail remains (figure 33). Carefully snip the tail close to the body, and gently tug the fabric until the remainder of the tail disappears.

FIGURE **33**

A MATTER OF STYLE

Style is a statement that is seen, not heard. As style relates to matters of fashion in everyday life, it is indeed the living, breathing picture that is worth a thousand words. I have had the pleasure and privilege of working with some of the top fashion stylists in the film, television, and print industries. I've watched these talented professionals use this silent language to speak volumes, without ever saying a word.

The language of style is made up of combinations of color, texture, mood, and arrangement. Accenting your wardrobe with crocheted accessories that you have made by hand is a wonderful way for you to convey your own personal style. Even the most traditional of all crochet patterns—the granny square—becomes a showstopper with a bold color scheme and forms the perfect complement for the casual fashionista.

Never underestimate the power of a single accessory. Minimalist jewelry and a crocheted hair ornament can create a feeling of understated grace and elegance.

special crochet stitches

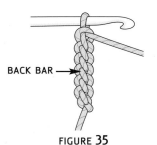

BACK LOOP   TOP TWO LOOPS   FRONT LOOP

FIGURE 34

BACK BAR →

FIGURE 35

WORKING IN (FRONT OR BACK) LOOPS AND BARS

Usually crochet stitches are worked under the two top loops of a stitch. However, you can achieve certain textural effects and shaping by working in the front or back loops only (figure 34), in the back bars of the foundation chain, or even in the spaces between stitches.

Certain stitch effects, such as the ribbing in Flaming Ribs and Char-Cowl, are achieved by working in either the front or back loops only.

Sometimes stitches are worked in the spaces between stitches rather than in the tops of the stitches, as in Flapper Gal and Chapeau L'Orange. This can create a more stretchy fabric—perfect for hats.

Occasionally stitches are worked under the back bars of the foundation chain (figure 35), as in Dragonfly Tote. This is often done to create a tight corner when working in the round.

PATTERN STITCHES

The basic crochet stitches are all you need to get started. However, combining the basic crochet stitches into pattern stitches takes your work to the next level. Many of the projects in this book use simple pattern stitches to create intriguing and attractive textures and lacey effects. While these "combination stitches" may sound complicated, they are simply a grouped working of the basics.

Here is a guide to of the textures and lace effects you will find in the projects in this book. You can find the details for making each of these stitch patterns in the individual project instructions.

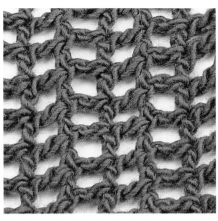

DOUBLE CROCHET MESH

DOUBLE CROCHET MESH

The mesh-like pattern in the Ruffled Roundabout Wrap is achieved by alternating double crochet and chain stitches.

SEED STITCH

Very different textures are created with similar placement of crochet stitches in the Two-Toned Tote and Pretty in Pink. The substantial texture of alternating ridges and openings in Two-Toned Tote is created by working two half double crochet stitches in every other stitch. Columns of lacey V's in Pretty in Pink are created by working two double crochet stitches in every other space between stitches.

THE ANGLED SHELL STITCH

Shell-like groupings of double crochet stitches are angled in alternating rounds about the Angled Shell Pompom Hat. Four double crochet stitches, two chain stitches, and another double crochet stitch are all worked in every fourth space between stitches.

SEED STITCH

THE ANGLED SHELL STITCH

OVERLAPPING DC3TOG

THE BOBBLE STITCH

THE RIB STITCH

OVERLAPPING DC3TOG

Typically a dc3tog (double crochet 3 stitches together) decreases the number of stitches in a round or row. In the Ruffled Roundabout Color-Block Scarf the dc3tog stitches are overlapped; the last double crochet of a previous dc3tog overlaps with the first double crochet of the next dc3tog, so the number of stitches is not decreased. Instead a fascinating texture is created.

THE BOBBLE STITCH

Bright dots of color adorn the Bobbled Messenger Bag. The bobbles are formed by changing the yarn color and working multiple double crochets into the same stitch. This bag is also felted, which provides the fleecy finish.

THE RIB STITCH

Long, slimming, stretchy ribbing is created by working stitches in the front loops only in the Flaming Rib Scarf.

CROSSED DOUBLE CROCHET

The rippled, almost leafy, texture in Jardin is produced by crossing double crochet stitches over each other.

SHELL STITCH

Grouping double crochet stitches can form a shell-like shape. The shells are then worked one on top of another, suggesting long winding paths so appropriate for Get Lost, an ultra-long scarf.

V-STITCH

V-stitches—groupings of double crochets separated by a chain—are a decorative way to increase the number of stitches in a round, as in Wineberry Kiss.

CROSSED DOUBLE CROCHET

SHELL STITCH

V-STITCH

special techniques

There is great beauty in simple crocheted pieces. Simple stitches + good color combinations + appropriately textured yarn make up the perfect equation for a smashing project. Doubling up, i.e. holding two different strands of yarn together while working, allows you to create custom color effects for your projects. I've also chosen to take many of the projects in this book to the next level in terms of design by adding some simple yet stylish details. It's really not that hard to go beyond the basics—and while the designs are beyond basic, the techniques used to execute them are quite simple and easy to learn. With the use of basic felting techniques, as well as embellishment with pompoms, tassels, and felt appliqué, you can create extraordinary accessories for yourself and your loved ones.

DOUBLING UP

Several of the pieces in the upcoming project section were created with two strands of yarn held together. This is a really fantastic, fun, fast way to create your own color blends and enhance the texture of a crocheted design. Just think: You can work a metallic yarn along with your next merino project or run a soft strand of super fluffy mohair with your next budget acrylic handbag. The options are endless and completely up to you and your imagination.

When holding two strands together, the extra weight and ply increase the sturdiness and overall durability of your crocheted garment, making it the perfect technique to use when fashioning handbags and totes. Doubling up greatly extends the lifespan of any crocheted garment, especially if it is not likely to be handled gently. It also increases the speed at which your crocheted piece is worked. Remember, though, that the increased weight and ply will call for the use of a larger hook.

BASIC FELTING

Felting is a process of controlled agitation that initially results in the swelling, intertwining, and ultimately the shrinkage of strands of natural fiber. If you have ever seen people with locked hair, often referred to as "dreadlocks," you were actually looking at a style achieved through felting. While I won't go into the details of felting (or locking) your hair, I can tell you how to felt the Bobbled Messenger Bag (or almost any other crocheted piece worked up with a natural felt-able fiber).

1. To begin the felting process, place your crocheted piece in a zippered lingerie bag or pillow protector case. Placing the crocheted piece in a protective casing aids in the felting process while guarding your washing machine against lint buildup.

2. Using hot water, a low water level setting, and laundry detergent, set your machine on its highest level of agitation. Place the piece to be felted, along with an old pair of jeans, into the washtub. If the water is hot enough and the agitation is adequate, the felting process takes only about 15 minutes.

3. Once you are satisfied with the density and degree of shrinkage of your piece, remove it from the washer and rinse it until the water runs clear. For some washers, this process could take less than one cycle so check the progress regularly. For other washers, this process could take several cycles.

4. Carefully shape your felted piece and lay it on a sweater rack to dry.

POMPOM 101

I've tried many tried and true pompom making techniques and found many of them lacking and most of them far too brain-twisting and complicated, in light of the purpose. Some complicated processes are worthy of their end results if you are in the business of saving lives, such as ending hunger or creating world peace. However, I am only willing to go so far, and no further, when it comes to making pompoms.

All of this said, the simplest way to make pompoms (of any size you desire) begins by creating your own cardboard pompom maker.

MAKING A POMPOM

1. Cut two lifesaver-shaped cardboard circles in the desired size.

2. Snip a pie-shaped opening in each circle.

3. Holding the two circles together, wrap your yarn around the pompom maker until it is completely covered and as full as possible.

FIGURE 36

FIGURE 37

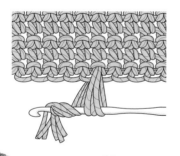

FIGURE 38

4. Use your scissors to snip through the loops of yarn you've made around the pompom maker (figure 36).

5. Take a length of yarn, slide it in between the two cardboard circles, and make a tight knot that ties the whole thing together (figure 37). I suggest wrapping and knotting the length of yarn more than once in order to properly secure the pompom.

6. Remove the pompom from the pompom maker, and trim it to shape with your scissors.

You can use the tail of the wrapped yarn to sew your finished pompom in place.

FRINGES

Adding a fringe to a crocheted piece has to be the easiest way to create a high-impact embellishment. Greater density and length always result in a more dramatic finished piece.

MAKING FRINGE

1. Decide on the desired fringe length, and cut a length of cardboard that is ½"/1.5cm longer than the desired fringe length.

2. Decide on the number of strands you would like to use for each fringe, multiply that by the number of fringes you intend to use, and wrap your yarn around the board that number of times.

3. Cut the loops off the board, and pick up the predetermined number of strands.

4. Fold the strands in half, and use the crochet hook to pull the folded end through the body of your crocheted piece.

5. Use the crochet hook to pull all of the strands of the fringe through the loop on the hook (figure 38).

6. Tighten your fringe by pulling on the cut ends.

7. Trim the fringe to even.

FAB-FELT APPLIQUÉ

Using ready-made felt squares is the perfect way to customize any crocheted piece. Embellishment options are virtually limitless. You can make roses, rabbits, apples, alligators, balloons, and butterflies, to name just a few. All it takes are some simple cutout shapes and a decent whipstitch to pull it off. Felt squares are readily available in a rainbow of colors at most craft stores.

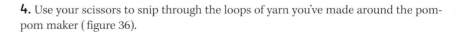

CREATING AN APPLIQUÉ:

1. Use a template that is ready-made, or sketch one of your own.

2. Cut pieces of felt into shapes according to your template.

3. Assemble your appliqué and glue or pin it in place.

4. Work a whipstitch around the edges to secure. Fasten off, weave in, and snip thread ends.

CARING FOR YOUR CROCHETED ITEMS

You've spent hours rummaging through bales of luxurious yarns. You've carefully hand-picked the perfect colors, weights, fiber combinations, and textures. You've lovingly labored through your project, hdc by hdc, as you've ridden the train back and forth and forth and back. You stand there holding your finished piece in the center of your prolific palms and ask yourself, "Now what?"

You may be thinking that your creative affair is over. The fact is that you have just given birth to a unique expression of your creative hand, and it needs a lifetime of care like any thing that is newly birthed.

My friend, it's not over. It has, indeed, just begun.

While manufacturers of yarn have clearly defined care recommendations printed on the labels, there are other factors to take into account. For example, you may have worked the body of a scarf in a hearty, no-fuss acrylic that you can toss into the washing machine on a high-heat setting; but what if you have embellished it with a high-maintenance, low-endurance extra-fine merino? The care recipe on the label is now a recipe for disaster.

When caring for handmade items into which you have lovingly poured your time and effort, I suggest taking a blanket approach of gentle lifetime care. Even when working with hearty, low-cost pieces, you can greatly extend their life and long-term condition by handling with extra care.

I suggest hand-washing all of your crocheted pieces with a very mild soap. Use minimal hand agitation and a lukewarm water temperature. After hand washing, rinse your piece in cold water until the water runs clear. Shake off the excess, and gently roll the piece in an absorbent, lint- free towel. Finally, carefully reshape the piece and lay it on a sweater net to dry.

As an added lint-evasive measure, you might consider storing your valued crocheted pieces in lingerie pouches.

ACKNOWLEDGMENTS

I thank my Lord and Savior, Jesus Christ, for blessing me with a loving and creative mother (Dixie), with a disciplined and dedicated husband (Moussa), with loving and supportive sons (Tiassa, Kouadio, and Kouassi), with a loving best friend (Lisa), and with a patient and understanding editor (Valerie).

ABOUT THE AUTHOR

As the owner of Afrigenix Salon in Manhattan's trendy Upper West Side, Francine Toukou has toured internationally as hair designer to a well-rounded roster of celebrity clients. She has studied design at the Fashion Institute of Technology and is also a craft instructor at New York City's Cutting Edge, and Knit Together, Get Together (a circle of fiber artists who create blankets to distribute to the homeless). Her work has been sold at New York's Museum of Arts & Design, in her West 72nd Street store, and at a number of small boutiques throughout the country.

INDEX